THE OHIO STATE
BAR ASSOCIATION
COLUMBUS, JAN. 25, 1924

OHIO STATE BAR ASSOCIATION
125ᵀᴴ ANNIVERSARY

The Ohio State Bar Association Mission Statement

OUR CORE PURPOSE:

To advance the professional interests of members of the Ohio State Bar Association

OUR CORE VALUES:

Member satisfaction, professionalism, foresight and quality services and products

OUR GOAL:

To make membership in the Ohio State Bar Association indispensable to Ohio lawyers

The Ohio State Bar Association would like to thank the following organizations for contributing to OSBA's 125th anniversary and making it possible to publish this pictorial history book:

OBLIC

Ohio Bar Liability
Insurance Company

OHIO STATE BAR ASSOCIATION. CLE INSTITUTE

OHIO STATE BAR ASSOCIATION INSURANCE AGENCY, INC.

*Frank***Gates** HIGHER GROUND

BUCKEYE BARRISTERS

A HISTORY OF THE

OHIO STATE BAR ASSOCIATION

EST 1880

125 YEARS OF SERVICE TO THE LEGAL PROFESSION

THE
DONNING COMPANY
PUBLISHERS

Special appreciation to William R. Van Aken for the original comprehensive 100-year history he and his colleagues prepared in 1980 that served as the foundation for this 125-year edition.

Julia A. Osborne, Esq., Author

Contributing editors for the 2005 edition of *Buckeye Barristers* include:

Richard C. Bannister
Kenneth A. Brown, Esq.
Colleen Buggy
Debby Cooper
Denny L. Ramey
Nina Sferra
William K. Weisenberg, Esq.

*   *   *

Copyright © 2005 by Ohio State Bar Association

All rights reserved, including the right to reproduce this work in any form whatsoever without permission in writing from the publisher, except for brief passages in connection with a review. For information, please write:

The Donning Company Publishers
184 Business Park Drive, Suite 206
Virginia Beach, Virginia 23462-6533

Steve Mull, *General Manager*
Barbara Buchanan, *Office Manager*
Kathleen Sheridan, *Senior Editor*
Dan Carr and Andrea L. W. Eisenberger, *Graphic Designers*
Stephanie Bass and Lynn Parrott, *Imaging Artists*
Mary Ellen Wheeler, *Proofreader*
Scott Rule, *Director of Marketing*
Travis Gallup, *Marketing Coordinator*
Anne Cordray, *Project Research Coordinator*

Dennis Walton, *Project Director*

Library of Congress Cataloging-in-Publication Data

Osborne, Julia L.
    Buckeye barristers : 125 years of service : a history of the Ohio State Bar Association / by Julia L. Osborne.
        p. cm.
    ISBN 1-57864-300-7 (alk. paper)
    1. Ohio State Bar Association—History. 2. Bar associations—Ohio—History. I. Title.

kf332.o35.o3546 2005
340'.06'0771—dc22
2005000480

Published in the United States of America by Walsworth Publishing Company

contents

preface

Heather G. Sowald, Columbus, representative of the 2001–2004 OSBA Board of Governors; OSBA president, 2004–2005.

AS A VISITING JUDGE FOR OHIO'S COMMON PLEAS courts, Hon. Richard M. Markus does not mince words. "The Ohio State Bar Association," he says, "provides greater services to its members than any other organization." Markus, who was president of the Association in 1991–1992, retired from his position as senior litigator for Porter Wright Morris and Arthur, Cleveland, in 1998 and works now about half-time, serving on the bench in 27 counties throughout the state. He goes on to say of the Association, "Its activities are unheard of in other states."

Ohio lawyers and other legal professionals generally agree with this characterization of the Ohio State Bar Association. The voluntary Association represents approximately 26,000 members of the bench and bar in Ohio, as well as nearly 5,000 law students and 550 paralegals.

According to attorney Thomas M. Taggart, of counsel to Vorys, Sater, Seymour and Pease, Columbus, and president of the Association for the 1997–1998 term, the organization is "more entrepreneurial and more forward-thinking in terms of services to its members than any other association I know. And it has been equally strong in thinking of ways to increase non-dues revenue.... A very significant percentage of Ohio lawyers look to it for all sorts of services."

At the ripe old age of 125, the Association is more active than ever. The organization that had its beginnings in a meeting hall in Cleveland in March 1880 has evolved into one of the strongest bar associations in the United States with clear and comprehensive services for all attorneys who choose to join, with a commitment to providing the public with legal information—and with a vision for the future.

Services to all

Both the young lawyer needing to find a particular cite to seal a position on a first case and the seasoned practitioner who wants

Kathleen B. Burke, Cleveland, representative of the 1989–1992 OSBA Board of Governors; OSBA president, 1993–1994.

BELOW: Keith A. Ashmus, Cleveland, representative of the 1998–2001 OSBA Board of Governors; OSBA president, 2003–2004.

to meet with peers and discuss general legal philosophies are well served by the Association. It offers new research techniques as well as strong advice and assistance to the legislature regarding issues of importance to the legal community. It serves both its members and the public by promoting high standards in the administration of justice and the practice of law.

Others familiar with the Association point to more positives. "I first joined in '75 or '76," says Kathleen B. Burke, a partner with Jones Day, Cleveland, who became the group's first female president in 1993. "One of the senior partners here got me involved." Burke says, "The group improves the public perception of lawyers, not just with public relations campaigns, but with activities that help increase the public understanding of the law. It helps make the legal system accessible to all."

Burke still serves on two state bar committees while devoting additional time as an Ohio delegate to the American Bar Association. She continues, "The Association helps lawyers to become familiar with, and take advantage of, the technology that's now available in practice." She cites in particular the Casemaker Web Library, an online legal research tool that provides attorneys with access to the law libraries of Ohio and numerous other states via computer.

Other longtime members praise the Association's legislative work. "The Association picks up on comprehensive initiatives and starts new ones," says Keith A. Ashmus, a partner with Frantz Ward, Cleveland, and president of the Association for the 2003–2004 term. "It's been a continuation of good works."

Organizations and benefits

Current Association President Heather G. Sowald, of Sowald, Sowald and Clouse, Columbus, has served on the Association's Council of Delegates since 1986. She began practicing law in 1979.

She notes the broad impact of the Association through its own programs and those of its affiliates. "The Ohio Bar Liability Insurance Company, with its complete insurance packages, and the Association's affordable and accessible continuing legal education classes let our lawyers take care of necessary requirements and focus on what's really important to them—the practice of law. The Association's goal is to make membership in it indispensable to Ohio lawyers. When they benefit, so do our justice system, our community and our families."

Other Association benefits include special programs and support for young lawyers, meetings and retreats, an annual con-

Hon. Richard M. Markus, Cleveland, representative of the 1986–1989 OSBA Board of Governors; OSBA president, 1991–1992.

Denny L. Ramey, OSBA executive director.

vention, and even organized recreational travel. Its publications include the award-winning bimonthly *Ohio Lawyer* magazine and the weekly *Ohio State Bar Association Report,* published since 1928, as well as newsletters and numerous electronic publications. (The Ohio State Bar Association is the only association in the country to provide a weekly publication including case summaries, legislative reports, and other up-to-the-minute legal information to its members.)

Building appeal

The Association is housed in a comfortable yet sophisticated building that opened in 1991, steps away from a scenic riverbank and minutes from the state's capitol. A plaque just inside the three-story, Williamsburg-style structure praises the time and effort expended by Leslie W. Jacobs, the Association's president for the 1986–1987 year, to make the building a reality.

Jacobs, a partner with Thompson Hine, Cleveland, explains the philosophy behind the inviting structure. "This was going to be our home," he recalls. "We wanted it to feel that way when we walk in the door."

"This is a marvelous building," Burke says. "The building is conducive to improving the Association's operations. It has enhanced and helped many areas. For example, the technology growth that we have experienced simply would not have been possible" in the old offices.

"Complete credit" to the staff

No matter how grand the facility, the Association could not function without an experienced and adaptable staff. Denny L. Ramey, hired in March 1980 as assistant executive director, has served as executive director since July 1986. "I give complete credit to Denny Ramey for our position today," Markus says simply. Taggart agrees that because of Ramey's leadership, the Association is "forward-thinking, solving problems before they become problems."

Ramey, the first executive director who is a certified association executive (CAE) rather than an attorney, came to the Association with seven years of professional association work behind him. The Portsmouth native, who is active in the National Association of Bar Executives, received his MBA from Capital University.

Richard C. Bannister, OSBA assistant executive director for administration.

Ramey is modest but honest about the Association's growth under his leadership. "In 1987," he says, "we began to look at the Association from a business standpoint. We were able to solidify the membership, and the lawyers liked being part of that. They took pride in the organization and pride in themselves." That has helped it evolve into a cutting-edge organization.

Ramey points to the Casemaker Web Library, an easy-to-use legal research tool that is now available to members as part of regular dues and has grown rapidly since the Association contracted with Lawriter LLC to offer Casemaker to other bar associations across the country. A Casemaker Consortium of 20 member states now shares the legal libraries of all the member states. "I've been in association management for more than 30 years, and Casemaker is the best membership benefit I have ever seen any association—bar or otherwise—provide its members," he notes.

Rick Bannister, the Association's assistant executive director for administration, is a native of Westerville who joined in June 2000. He says of the Association's reputation, "Over its 125-year history, and most certainly over the past 25 years, the Association has been one of the leading bar associations in the country. It has earned its reputation by staying committed to a very simple, core goal: 'To be indispensable to Ohio lawyers.'"

At home in the House (and Senate)

William K. Weisenberg, the Association's assistant executive director of public affairs and government relations and chief lobbyist, has coordinated and implemented legislative work on behalf of Ohio's legal profession since 1979, with significant triumphs. For example, the state now permits the formation of limited liability companies and limited liability partnerships, has made sweeping changes to domestic relations law, and has implemented a modernization of the general corporation law.

When Weisenberg, a New York City native, graduated from New York Law School in 1969, he was offered an opportunity to serve in Cleveland or Columbus as a Volunteer in Service to America (VISTA) lawyer. He chose Columbus, where he worked with social service agencies serving the indigent.

After one year of service, he joined a law firm and then worked for the state of Ohio in several positions. In 1972, he began lobbying the Ohio Legislature on behalf of several government agencies. He served as counsel to the Ohio House

William K. Weisenberg, OSBA assistant executive director of public affairs and government relations.

Judiciary Committee and left that position to join the Association in 1979.

He works with Association committees as they draft potential legislation, then arranges for the drafts to be reviewed by the Council of Delegates and the Association Board of Governors. Next, he works with state legislators to find a sponsor or sponsors for the bill and meets with lawmakers to discuss the positives and negatives of any potential piece of legislation.

When the Association opposes a bill, Weisenberg is the one to call the problems to the legislators' attention. If necessary, he also arranges for Association members to testify regarding potential actions.

Legislative actions that have been taken on Weisenberg's watch include comparative negligence; revision of custody laws in divorce; corporate and business anti-takeover legislation; modifications to processing medical liability claims; avoidance of taxation of legal services; establishment of the Ohio Legal Assistance Foundation; and funding for civil services, among many other actions.

He received the Ohio Legal Assistance Foundation Presidential Award in 1997; the Ohio Lobbying Association President's Award in 1998; and the Ohio State Bar Foundation Award for Outstanding Research or Service in Law or Government in 2000.

Weisenberg was honored for his 25 years of service in 2004; Ramey was honored in 2005. "Both men have exemplified high integrity, ethics, leadership and vision for the benefit of this organization and its members," Sowald says. "Each has worked extremely hard to make the Association into what I believe to be the top state bar association in the country. We have been very fortunate to have them, their wisdom and their experience at the helm of our organization," she continues, "and we will, hopefully, have them at the helm for many years to come."

Key concerns

Hot issues that the Association has tackled in the last 25 years include a bitter battle with the Supreme Court of Ohio in the mid-'80s. At the same time, the Association has lobbied long and hard over the years for merit selection of judges instead of traditional elections but has yet to impact voters on this issue.

Leslie W. Jacobs, Cleveland, representative of the 1983–1985 OSBA Board of Governors; OSBA president, 1986–1987.

Money management

Solid financial decisions and management, including the 1998 sale of Ohio Professional Electronic Network (later the Online Professional Electronic Network or OPEN) for a $6 million profit and the 1999 sale of the Ohio Bar Title Insurance Co. by the Ohio State Bar Foundation for $19 million have allowed the Association the luxury of offering numerous services to its members and the public without prohibitive costs.

It is with pride that Taggart, Burke and others represent the Ohio State Bar Association at meetings of the American Bar Association. Taggart says, "When I meet with other presidents and leaders, I realize we don't have their problems. I realize we're way ahead of the curve every time I go to a meeting."

What's ahead

Reaching its 125th anniversary gives the Association a chance to look back but no time to rest. "Now there are changes in technology," Markus says, "and, therefore, changes in communication and analysis…. The future specifics are beyond anyone's imagination." However, he believes the future must involve a continuing focus.

Legislation remains uppermost in the minds of other Association members. "The bar will have to work very hard in terms of providing information to voters about the way judges are selected," Burke says. "The bar will continue to take the lead in raising this issue and work toward an acceptable alternative to our current judicial election system."

John A. Carnahan, Columbus, representative of the 1977–1980 OSBA Board of Governors; OSBA president, 1983–1984.

Fundamentally, attorneys all over Ohio must be willing to work together for what is best for the profession, and the Association serves as the catalyst for change. "There are lawyers … and lawyers," says John A. Carnahan, the 1983–1984 president who retired from private practice in 1999 and is now in-house counsel to XLO Group, an automotive parts manufacturer in Cleveland. He draws a distinction between "small town offices" and "partners in big city law firms," explaining that although the needs of these two groups are very different, the Association brings them together.

"There's no end to our need to understand one another" through meetings and discussions, he says. "We also need to maintain, strengthen and pay heed to our professionalism…. Our relationship with our clients is a fiduciary relationship, with

Thomas M. Taggart, Columbus, representative of the 1991-1996 OSBA Board of Governors; OSBA president, 1997-1998.

Frank E. Bazler, Troy, representative of the 1979-1982 OSBA Board of Governors; OSBA president, 1984-1985.

elevated responsibility not only to our clients, but also a terrific responsibility to maintain our system of justice."

Sowald underscores the Association's need for future planning. "The Association must conduct a study of the future of the profession," she says. "We need to prepare ourselves, our profession and the Association for those inevitable and rapid changes in the way law will be practiced, and we need to ensure that the public will continue to have access to our justice system."

*   *   *

This 125-year history of the Ohio State Bar Association consists of two sections. In 1979, Cleveland attorney William R. Van Aken volunteered to compile information about the Association's first 100 years. Van Aken joined in 1938 and became its president in 1958. He also served as president of the Ohio State Bar Foundation from 1971 to 1976 and was one of the organizers of the National Conference of Bar Foundations. In 1975, he received the Association's most prestigious award, the Ohio Bar Medal, for his contributions.

Van Aken's 336-page softbound book, *Buckeye Barristers*, was distributed at the 1980 annual meeting and has long been out of print. Nonetheless, the Association still receives requests for it today 25 years later. The Association recognized him for his comprehensive work in a 1988 ceremony, presenting him with a special Ohio-shaped plaque with a buckeye attached to the Cleveland area.

Those who have requested *Buckeye Barristers* in the past should be pleased to know that it is now available through the Internet in its entirety. Check www.ohiobar.org for this wonderfully detailed report of annual meetings, leading personalities, concerns of the times and, yes, even descriptions of some amusing extracurricular activities of the bar.

Part I

Part I of the 2005 edition of *Buckeye Barristers* includes highlights from Van Aken's work, as well as some information about what was happening in Ohio and around the country during those first 100 years to put the current activities of the Association into context.

Buckeye Barristers

A Centennial History of
the Ohio State Bar Association
by William R. Van Aken

Part II

Part II provides information about the activities of the Association since Van Aken's work was published, including the establishment and/or growth of:

- Casemaker/OSBA.COM.LLC/Lawriter.LLC
- The Ohio State Bar Association CLE Institute
- The Ohio Center for Law-Related Education
- The Ohio Lawyers Assistance Program
- The Ohio State Legal Services Association
- The Ohio Professional Electronic Network (OPEN, which later became the Online Professional Electronic Network)
- The Ohio State Bar Foundation
- The Ohio Bar Liability Insurance Co.
- The Ohio State Bar Association Insurance Agency

The 2005 edition follows the re-establishment of *Ohio Lawyer* magazine in the 1980s and the planning and execution of the move from cramped and outdated quarters to an impressive new set of buildings created for the Association and its affiliates.

It describes the evolution of the Association logo and support of new legislation and new regulatory programs for the practice of law.

Perhaps most fundamentally, this book traces the events of what was, in the 1980s, a "bitter war" with Supreme Court of Ohio Chief Justice Frank Celebrezze and the justices who sided with him, and essentially a fight for the Association's survival. When this "war" was over, the Association had a few new heroes, newfound strength, and its members had many more stories to tell.

*   *   *

Some readers will remember decades of events in the Association's past. Others will discover historic events, large and small, for the first time. In either case, we hope that the past provides a solid base and a complete perspective for the Association's strong future and for the individuals who will work to fulfill its potential.

OPPOSITE: *Buckeye Barristers: A Centennial History*, written by William R. Van Aken, is a history of the OSBA's first 100 years. It is a 336-page softbound book that was distributed at the 1980 annual meeting.

part 1

COOPER K. WATSON.   GEO. W. HOUK.   DURBIN W

WM. WHITE.   THOS. E. POWELL.   SAM'L F.

SOME PROMINENT MEMBERS OF THE OHIO BAR. 1878

chapter 1

Ohio State Bar Association— First Steps

IT WAS 1775. THE MEMBERS OF THE BAR IN THE COL-
onies were well educated and well qualified. They stood high
in public esteem. But, a year later, with the beginning of the
American Revolution, conditions changed, and the legal
profession began a long period of decline.

One reason for the decline of the profession and the public
perception of it was that as many as a third of the colonial
lawyers remained loyal to the Crown and left the fledgling
country during, or immediately after, the hostilities.

The war brought freedom for the United States. It also
brought severe economic depression. Lawyers were responsible
for filing lawsuits to enforce unpaid debts, and this did nothing to
improve their public standing. Further, the mysteries and
intricacies of common law, borrowed largely from England,
caused even more disapproval and distrust.

By 1829, with the election of Andrew Jackson as the seventh
president of the United States, the popularity of the "common
man" seemed to reach its peak. By and large, lawyers were not seen
as "commoners" who championed the rights of their fellow
Americans. The fact that they were, of necessity, a better educated
group than those in most other professions at the time was not an
asset in the court of public perception.

In the 18th century, serious study
was required before anyone could
practice law. At the beginning of the 19th
century, 14 out of 19 states had definite
requirements for study in preparation
for admittance to the bar. Forty years
later, only 11 of 30 states had maintained
such standards, and by 1860, only nine of
39 had kept this prerequisite.

Some states even abolished all
educational requirements for admission
to the bar. In fact, Ohio's neighboring

OPPOSITE: **Some prominent members of the Ohio bar in 1878.**

BELOW: **The result of the Great Flood of 1884 on W. Third Street in Cincinnati.**

(*Ohio Historical Society*)

> **Good laws lead to the making of better ones; bad ones bring about worse. As soon as any man says of the affairs of the State, "What does it matter to me?" the State may be given up for lost.**
>
> —*Jean Jacques Rousseau (1712–1778)*

state, Indiana, wrote into its constitution in 1851, "Every person of good moral character who is a voter is entitled to practice law in any of the courts of the state."

Mr. Schuester, I presume?

Just before the Civil War, lawyers may have inadvertently helped add another, albeit negative, word to the dictionary. One story goes that a New York City attorney named Schuester so enraged a judge with his underhanded techniques that the judge began to reprimand other lawyers for their "Schuester" practices. "Schuester" was shortened to "shyster," and the name stuck.

By 1870, legitimate lawyers were spending most of their time—and the courts' time—correcting the mistakes of unqualified practitioners. Dealing with hearse chasers (the ambulance chasers of their day) filled more courtroom hours, while other lawyers took advantage of procedural intricacies to trap defendants and stall plaintiffs.

That same year, New York City was firmly in the grip of the Tweed ring, with thieveries from the public treasury both blatant and enormous. William Marcy "Boss" Tweed was a lawyer, and three judges were involved in the misdeeds. Lawyers from New York City hatched a plan to form the first organized bar association to purge the profession of dishonest lawyers and judges—and to crack the Tweed ring.

The result of the Ohio Flood in 1884.
(*Ohio Historical Society*)

Now is the time for all good men to come
to the aid of their country

One of the founders of the Association of the Bar of the City of New York (founded in 1870) stated that its first order of business was to "restore the honor, integrity and fame of the profession in its manifestations of the Bench and of the Bar." Following a series of prosecutions, disbarments and forced resignations from the bar, the Tweed ring lost its power, and the public took note. It was in this same time period that lawyers in other states were realizing the benefits of organized bar associations—to serve the legal profession as well as the public.

In Ohio, the Franklin County Bar Association was formed in 1869; the Cincinnati Bar Association followed three years later. The Cleveland Bar Association was formed a year behind that; Akron followed in 1875; and Toledo in 1878. Across the United States, state bar associations began to take shape. The New Hampshire Bar Association became a reality in 1873; bar associations in the District of Columbia, Iowa, Connecticut, New York State, and Iowa followed within a few years. The American Bar Association came into being in 1878.

The year 1878 was important for the future of the state and the nation since it was the same year that William Howard Taft graduated from the University of Cincinnati Law School. Two years later, the Ohio State Bar Association was founded.

A meeting of the Butler County
Bar Association in 1897.

REPORT

OF THE

CONVENTION,

HELD AT

CLEVELAND, JULY 8TH AND 9TH, 1880,

FOR THE PURPOSE OF FORMING A

STATE BAR ASSOCIATION.

CLEVELAND, O:
HOME COMPANION PUBLISHING CO,
1880.

REMINISCENCES OF THE

Early Judges, Courts and Members of the Bar of Ohio.

AN ADDRESS

TO THE

STATE BAR ASSOCIATION OF OHIO

AT THE

Annual Meeting, Columbus, Dec. 26, 1883.

BY

Hon. HENRY B. CURTIS.

THE OHIO STATE
ARCHAEOLOGICAL AND HISTORICAL
SOCIETY LIBRARY

COLUMBUS:
OHIO LAW PUBLISHING COMPANY
1884

ABOVE LEFT: The Report of the OSBA's first convention held in Cleveland.

ABOVE RIGHT: A publication by Henry B. Curtis that was delivered at the 1883 OSBA Annual Meeting.

(*Ohio Historical Society*)

RIGHT: Put-in-Bay was the site of the Association's summer annual meeting for 21 years.
(*Ohio Historical Society*)

The million dollar Perry Memorial Monument

Put-in-Bay
America's Most Unique
Island Resort

chapter 2

Beginnings of the Ohio State Bar Association

MARCH 6, 1880, MARKED THE BIRTH OF THE OHIO State Bar Association when the Cleveland Bar Association's Executive Committee adopted the following resolution: "It is the sense of this Association that a State Bar Association be formed and that the Corresponding Secretary correspond with the various city and county associations in the State upon the subject to obtain if possible their cooperation."

Invitations went out to local bar associations throughout the state, and more than 400 lawyers gathered in Case Hall in Cleveland on July 8, 1880, to lay the foundation for the Ohio State Bar Association. Case Hall was the cultural center of Cleveland and had in previous years played host to Mark Twain, Harriet Beecher Stowe, Horace Greeley, Susan B. Anthony, Thomas Nast and others.

Rufus P. Ranney, born in Massachusetts in 1813 and a resident of Portage County, Ohio, since 1822, was to become the Ohio State Bar Association's first president. In 1850, he became a justice of the Supreme Court of Ohio but resigned six years later and made an unsuccessful bid for Ohio governor in 1859. He again served as justice of the Supreme Court of Ohio and again resigned in 1865, this time to practice law in Cleveland. He died in 1891.

Ranney was one of the attorneys who in 1880 issued the call for the Case Hall meeting. He had already established himself as a leader of the Ohio bar and was chosen to deliver the welcoming address at Case Hall.

At the meeting, he outlined the purposes of the proposed state bar, underscored the responsibility of lawyers, and listed what the members of the legal profession must do to be faithful to their trust. He emphasized that the profession had a duty to police itself, and his remarks echoed for the next 100 years or so.

Case Hall was the site of the first meeting of the Ohio State Bar Association in July, 1880. Built in 1867, it stood on the northwest corner of Superior Avenue and East Third Street in Cleveland, and was the cultural center of the city for twenty years. This drawing by artist Donald W. Pickas was taken from a contemporary woodcut.

Rufus P. Ranney, first OSBA president.

Among Ranney's remarks: "If you will reflect for a single moment that the duties of the lawyer are simply a succession and combination of trusts reposed in him by others, it will then be apparent to you that you all should be faithful to your trusts...." and "What is it that the members of the bar and the gentlemen upon the bench are called upon constantly to deal with and administer? One of the grandest sciences known in the whole list, an applied science—applied a thousand times every day to the concerns of men in society...." Of course, he was speaking of the law.

The newly formed Association set a $2 annual membership fee and described its purpose as follows:

The association is formed to advance the science of jurisprudence, to promote reform in the law, to facilitate the administration of justice, to uphold integrity, honor and courtesy in the legal profession, to encourage thorough liberal legal education and to cultivate cordial intercourse among the members of the bar.

As president, Ranney was supported by many vice presidents, including R.P. Buckland, Fremont; Leander J. Critchfield, Columbus; Luther Day, Ravenna; D. Dirlan, Mansfield; D.A. Hollingsworth, Cadiz; George W. Houk, Dayton; Samuel S. Knowles, Marietta; William Lawrence, Bellefontaine; Stanley Matthews, Cincinnati; and Henry Newbegin, Defiance. Columbus resident J.T. Holmes was elected secretary, and W.J. Boardman of Cleveland was chosen to be treasurer.

It had been requested that each county send one lawyer for each 10 in the county, but many sent more. Of the 400 lawyers present at the Case Hall meeting, 164 were accredited delegates to the convention.

The group concluded its first business meeting and set its next meeting for Dec. 28, 1880, in Columbus. At that meeting, William McKinley Jr.—who became Stark County prosecutor, congressman, governor of Ohio, and president of the United States—was nominated for membership, as was William R. Day, who became secretary of state and later was appointed to the U.S. Supreme Court.

The following meeting was set for July 1881 but was postponed and held later the same year in Toledo. It was especially significant because bylaws were adopted to support the Association's constitution and Rufus King was elected its second president. The Association now had 391 members.

chapter 3

The Early Years

IN THE EARLY 1880s, OHIO'S FAVORITE SONS DOMI-nated the national political scene. Former governor and President Rutherford B. Hayes had been elected to his third term as governor in 1876 but resigned in 1877 to run for the presidency. He served only one term, and fellow Ohioan and former Congressman James A. Garfield replaced him as commander in chief. Supreme Court Chief Justice Morrison R. Waite, Toledo, administered the oath of office to Garfield. Gens. Philip H. Sheridan and William T. Sherman, along with Sherman's brother, former Sen. John Sherman, by then the secretary of the treasury, witnessed the event.

The first proposed legislation

For the first decade of the Ohio State Bar Association's history, annual meetings were convened at various locations throughout the state. Columbus, Toledo, Cincinnati, Dayton, Springfield and Toledo hosted these meetings, generally held at the end of each calendar year. Agenda items of those times resemble many still considered at Association annual meetings today.

There was much concern then, as now, over delays in the courts, and the first piece of legislation the Association suggested to the Ohio Legislature was a plan for streamlining the process. The plan noted that common pleas judges also sat as district court justices for the purpose of reviewing the decisions of the trial court. This meant that often the judges were reviewing their own decisions, and more and more cases were finding their way to the Supreme Court of Ohio. The Association's solution was to abolish the district courts.

While the legislature granted the Association a joint hearing, nothing more came of the proposed plan. Soon after the hearing, the Association suggested increasing the size of the Supreme Court of Ohio and replacing district courts with circuit courts. The state legislature agreed and adopted the plan. It was put to a

An early photo of the justices of the Supreme Court of Ohio.

vote of the people and soon became law. The newly minted circuit courts received quick praise, but the timeliness of Supreme Court of Ohio hearings continued to be an issue for the Ohio State Bar Association.

Competency and other issues

A second recurring issue the Association sought to address was the competency of members of the bar. One president noted, "The bar is judged harshly, perhaps overmuch, by its lower edge." A few years later, an Association member suggested that attorneys should receive a more thorough education and that there should be a probationary period for all applicants before they could become full practitioners. In 1889, Association President J.J. Moore, Ottawa, summarized the feeling of members that they needed to police their profession. "We can elevate the standards of the lawyers by being more severe in our methods." He suggested individual members should "purge" the profession of its incompetent and unscrupulous members, and he charged local bar associations with this task.

The issue of press relations was a third concern, voiced for the first time by Association members in 1883. However, there was no strategy for dealing with this issue. "The best way to meet newspaper reports is to ignore them," said one faction of the group. One member (and future Association president), Stephen R. Harris, Bucyrus, dismissed a particular criticism of the bar by saying, "We all know that the writer of these articles evidently did not know what he was talking about...." Press relations and the public image of lawyers would continue to be an issue, and the Association would look for ways to address it in later years.

Supreme quarters

During the late 1880s, Association members first began to discuss the inadequacy of the quarters of the Supreme Court of Ohio and the state's law library. One suggestion was to establish the Department of Justice at the Statehouse and to house the Supreme Court, the Law Library and the Attorney General's Office in a separate building. These issues were resolved in 1913, and the construction of the Judicial Annex to the Statehouse began.

Association's early membership woes

The Association had some internal concerns in its early years. In 1886, for example, it had $260.15 in its treasury, a figure that had only increased to $317.35 by the end of that year. Though 543 lawyers were now Association members, 118 of them who had paid their initiation fees had not bothered to follow up with annual payment of dues (which continued to be $2 per year). There was not a financial crisis, but there was much irritation with the fact that some non-paying members were reaping the same benefits as other dues-paying members. The solution was to drop from the rolls those who had not paid in a year.

Putting in at Put-in-Bay

Put-in-Bay was chosen as the site for the 1888 annual meeting, and though the custom had been to rotate locations, the meeting was such a success that Put-in-Bay was chosen as the site for the next 21 years.

The year 1888 also marked the ascendancy of yet another Buckeye to the top government office in the country. Benjamin Harrison was a senator from Indiana, but he had been born in North Bend, Ohio, at the home of his grandfather, William Henry

LEFT: Kenyon College and Harvard Law graduate Rutherford B. Hayes was elected to his third term as governor of Ohio in 1876 but resigned to run for the office of U.S. president. He promised he would serve only one term and did so, from 1877 to 1881. Fellow Ohioan James A. Garfield replaced him as commander in chief. Hayes retired to Fremont, Ohio, where he died in 1893.

BELOW: Former Ohio Congressman James A. Garfield became the 20th president of the United States on March 4, 1881. On July 2, 1881, Charles Guiteau, an embittered attorney who had sought an appointed office, shot him at a Washington, D.C., railroad station. Garfield died Sept. 19, 1881. One of his seven children, James R. Garfield, was later active in the Association and went on to become Ohio state senator and secretary of the interior under President Theodore Roosevelt. (*Ohio Historical Society*)

FARMER GARFIELD
Cutting a Swath to the White House.

BREAKERS HOTEL
Cedar Point, Ohio

When Put-in-Bay was forsaken as its meeting-place, the Ohio State Bar Association chose the Breakers Hotel at the famous Cedar Point resort near Sandusky as the site for most of its annual meetings from 1910 to 1934. Photo courtesy of the Ohio Historical Society.

Harrison. William McKinley and Secretary John Sherman also had been candidates for the position, and Sherman ultimately became Harrison's vice president. In an eerily familiar precursor to more recent elections, Harrison did not get a majority of the popular vote but garnered enough electoral votes to win the presidency.

A key concern for the Association in 1888 was how it might participate in the Ohio Centennial celebration, set for Sept. 19, 1888, in Columbus. Yet as late as July 1888, the Association had still not decided what to do. It quickly appointed a committee that wrote speeches and prepared music, and the show went on, complete with a rendition of *Auld Lang Syne* at the conclusion of the statewide event.

The year 1889 held a special significance: It was the first time that a woman would join the Association. Nettie Cronise was born in Republic, Ohio, on Sept. 26, 1843. After her parents' divorce, Nettie's grandfather adopted her and her younger sister, Florence. Nettie attended Heidelberg College in Tiffin until an eye problem forced her to withdraw. She earned her bachelor's degree from the State Normal School of Illinois, then taught for several years in Peru, Illinois. In 1869, Nettie returned to Tiffin and continued teaching.

Nettie and Florence began to read law in different law offices in Tiffin in 1871. On April 4, 1873, after examination by the District Court in Tiffin, Nettie was admitted to the Ohio bar over vigorous opposition. She immediately entered practice and was successful from the start. Ohio's second woman lawyer, Florence Cronise, was admitted in September 1873, and the two

Nettie Cronise Lutes (pictured here) and her sister, Florence Cronise, Tiffin, were the first women to be admitted to the Ohio bar.

practiced as "N. & F. Cronise." Their broad general practice was the longest continuous practice of the first generation of American women lawyers. Nettie married former classmate Nelson B. Lutes (1848–1900) in 1874, and they had three daughters. Nettie, Florence, and Nelson were admitted to the U.S. District Court in Toledo in 1879.

Nettie left her partnership with Florence in 1880 and began to practice with Nelson as "Lutes and Lutes." Nelson, a Civil War veteran, began to lose his hearing in the late 1870s. By 1881, he was completely deaf, so Nettie became Nelson's "ears." Nelson did all the speaking in court; Nettie mouthed to him what was being said. They came to specialize in corporate work in both state and federal courts in Ohio, Michigan and Indiana. In 1898, Nettie and Nelson were admitted to the U.S. District Court in Indianapolis.

Nettie and Florence let their Association membership lapse after only a couple of years. After Nelson died, Nettie practiced alone until her daughter, Evelyn, was admitted to the bar in 1905. Mother and daughter resurrected the old "Lutes and Lutes" shingle until Nettie retired in 1917 due to ill health. Nettie died in Tiffin on July 31, 1923.

chapter 4

A New Decade

SOMEONE READING ABOUT THE ASSOCIATION'S concerns in the "'90s" might be uncertain which century was being discussed. Hot topics in the 1890s included the increasing number of divorce cases, judges' wages and, prominently, attorney advertising.

In other state news, the voters first had the option of secret ballots. Previously, they simply told election clerks how to record their votes. The new law required paper ballots and ballot boxes.

Your comments, Mr. McKinley

Then-Governor William McKinley, who had been an Association member since its first year, delivered a welcoming address to the Association in 1892. His words then might well be spoken today. "The [legal] profession," he said, "is essential to civilization. It touches every relation in life…. The lawyer holds the secrets of his clients…. There is no profession where honor and integrity are at a higher premium than in the profession of the law."

President Harrison had lost the 1892 election, and Grover Cleveland reassumed the office. McKinley had been reelected as governor during a problematic time in the history of the state, known as the "Panic of 1893." The federal government was buying silver from western states and cutting the amount of gold in the U.S. Treasury. Banks failed, businesses closed and the unemployed had nothing to spend to improve the economy. The federal legislation that was blamed for the problem was repealed soon after, but it still took another four years for Ohio's economy to recover.

Famous for their participation as Association members in 1893 were James R. Garfield, a future member of the president's cabinet, and his brother, Harry R. Garfield (both sons of the late James A. Garfield).

McKinley's opponent in his bid for the presidency in the 1896 election was Congressman William Jennings Bryan, who was

Cleveland lawyers could soon invite their colleagues and clients to "see the light," literally, as the first power station in the United States was opened in Euclid in 1881.

known for his oratory and spent much of his time speaking throughout the country. In contrast, McKinley spoke from his front porch in Canton to groups of fellow Republicans. (Warren G. Harding, another Ohioan who rose to the country's highest office, used a similar successful strategy years later.)

After his election, McKinley had a very good reason for not attending the Association's annual meeting. Because he was then president of the United States and too busy to spend much time practicing law in Ohio, his status changed from regular to ex officio membership. President McKinley was not the only Association member to serve in Washington, D.C.; he had tapped another powerful member of the Association, Canton resident William R. Day, first as assistant, then as secretary of state.

Other key members

A member who attended the annual meetings in the late 1890s and wielded his own power was Judge George K. Nash, president of the Association in 1896–1897. Nash would later become the governor of the state, as would succeeding Association President Judson Harmon. A new member from Canton, Atlee Pomerene, would later gain fame as the prosecutor in the Teapot Dome scandals. (And J.E. Sater, with a name long famous in Ohio law in relation to his law firm, also joined the Association in 1897.)

The Spanish-American War

On April 20, 1898, the country became involved in the Spanish-American War. The first annual meeting to be held during a war was that year in Put-in-Bay, and Ohio was the first state to muster a volunteer regiment and place it in the field. By the end of the war, more than 15,000 Ohioans were serving in the military (though only three units actually ever left the United States). Day took over as secretary of state; after the war he became a U.S. Supreme Court justice.

The Association's president in 1897–1898, Hillsboro resident Judson Harmon, gave what was later described as a "statesman-like" address at the 1898 meeting. Rather than focus on specific Association issues, he took the time to talk about acquiring a territory by force if necessary, a position favored by some during the Spanish-American War. His comments focused on current events as well as the war, and he was later praised by other members for his easy-to-understand take on the immediate situation. He was bringing the "big picture" of national politics to Ohio lawyers.

Advertising issues

An 1896 committee report expressed grave concern about advertising by some lawyers in larger cities who held themselves out as specialists in personal injury and wrongful death actions and offered to represent injured parties for a contingent fee. The committee chairman complained, "Very many actions have been, and are being, commenced in our courts, without legal merit or foundation, for the sole purpose of extortion and for the purpose of compelling the payment of attorney fees...." The committee concluded that local bar associations needed to take action. This may have been the first time lawyer advertising was mentioned in the state, but it would by no means be the last time.

Low salaries

Salaries paid to judges were much discussed in the mid-'90s. This had been a problem for some time, as attested to by an earlier Association meeting speaker who told the story of a lawyer and his son who met an Ohio Supreme Court justice in Columbus. After the introduction, the justice went on his way, and the son asked his father, "Why did you call that man a judge?"

"Because he is a judge," the older man responded.

The son was skeptical. "I thought from his dress and personal appearance that he must be a farmer."

The point of the story, the speaker explained, was that the Ohio judge, excellent though he might be, was paid a farmer's wages. The Association passed at least two resolutions during the decade to urge the General Assembly to raise the salaries of Ohio Supreme Court justices to $6,000 per year. The state legislature granted this increase in 1902.

> "The law, wherein, as in a magic mirror, we see reflected not only our own lives, but the lives of all men that have been! When I think on this majestic theme, my eyes dazzle." —*Oliver Wendell Holmes, Jr. (1841–1935)*
>
> *to the Suffolk Bar Association (1885)*

Money and more

Finances played a key role in the early years of the Association, and every penny counted. This was especially true when members were still paying just $2 a year in dues. In 1897, the Association shelled out $1.25 for its first telephone bill. Other notable charges: in 1899, there was a 35-cent expense for shipping books to the annual meeting, and $295.50 was paid to print the annual report of the proceedings.

Law students still rue discussion that began in 1893 on increasing the scholastic requirements for admission to the bar from two to three years in law school. By the time of the next annual meeting, the three-year requirement had become a reality.

Annual meetings created opportunities to debate, discuss, plan and advise. Members of today's Board of Governors would be interested in the philosophy of its 1895 predecessor, the Executive Committee: "The object [of our] Committee is to provide for the entertainment of the members of the Association and for the order of business at the meeting."

If the dinner menu for the 1894 annual meeting was typical work of this committee, there was glorious (if overabundant) success. The menu included mock turtle soup, broiled whitefish, sweet breads, peas, tomatoes, broiled chicken, potatoes, shrimp salad, cake, ice cream, oranges, bananas, cheese and crackers. Drinks included wine, Champagne with the entrée, and coffee after dinner.

chapter 5

A New Century,
A New World

ONE OF THE SADDEST EVENTS FOR THE YOUNG Association was the death of one of its most well-known members. President William McKinley, who had become president of the United States in 1897 with the largest majority of popular votes since 1872, had begun a strong second term in 1901. However, in September of that year, while in a receiving line at the Buffalo Pan-American Exposition, he was shot twice by anarchist Leon Czolgosz (who spent much of his time before the assassination on a farm near Cleveland). McKinley died eight days later.

The Association planned a memorial for McKinley in 1903, two years after his death. The long-delayed memorial included an address written by personal friends of the lawyer-turned-politician.

McKinley Memorial.
(*Ohio Historical Society*)

RIGHT: The Ohio State Bar Association celebrated its 23rd anniversary as the state of Ohio celebrated its centennial. Shown is an elevated view of a crowd gathered on the street in Chillicothe, Ohio, after the Ohio Centennial parade on May 21, 1903.

BELOW: The Ohio Statehouse.

(*Ohio Historical Society*)

Future President William Howard Taft graduated from the University of Cincinnati Law School in 1878 and spoke to the Association as an ex-officio member at the annual convention in 1906. He is shown here descending from the speaker's platform during his presidential campaign on Taft Day in Cincinnati in 1908.

BELOW: Ohio lawyer William Howard Taft and his running mate, New Yorker James S. Sherman, shown on a presidential campaign postcard with the slogan, "The Nations Choice." Taft served as the 27th president from 1909 to 1913 and died in 1930; Sherman died in office in 1912.

(*Ohio Historical Society*)

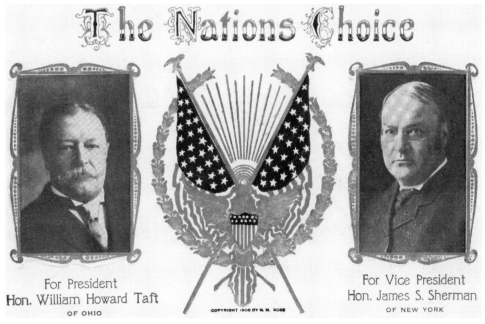

The Nations Choice

For President
Hon. William Howard Taft
OF OHIO

For Vice President
Hon. James S. Sherman
OF NEW YORK

The Supreme Court of Ohio justices in 1906.

Powerful Ohioans

Top officials other than President McKinley spoke at Association events during the first decade of the new century. In 1901, William R. Day of Canton, McKinley's secretary of state and Association member, spoke, as did James R. Garfield, Ohio state senator and son of President James A. Garfield. (The younger Garfield later became secretary of the interior under President Theodore Roosevelt.) Future president William Howard Taft, who was also an ex-officio member of the Association, spoke at the 1906 meeting, discussing the Panama Canal in depth.

Accomplishments of the first 25 years

The Association's 25th anniversary was celebrated at the annual convention at Put-in-Bay in 1905. The group's president proudly offered a list of suggestions that the Association had made and implemented in the furtherance of justice:

- Most important, an increase in the salaries of the Supreme Court justices and the construction of a better home for the Court in the new Statehouse Annex;
- Establishment of circuit courts to lighten the caseload of the Supreme Court;
- Improvement in the way jurors are selected;
- Strengthened veto power for the governor;
- Increase in training required for law students and a standardized bar exam;
- Codification of criminal law as well as domestic relations and negotiable instruments; and
- Adoption of the municipal code.

Because it was necessary for the day-to-day work of lawyers, Supreme Court of Ohio decisions were published on a regular if infrequent basis. In 1904, the Supreme Court reporter noted proudly that, in recent years, the number of reports had increased to two per year.

Legal ethics continued to be a significant issue in the first decade of the 20th century. An American Bar Association committee, including some of the country's top lawyers, put together a comprehensive Canon of Ethics that was adopted at its annual meeting in 1908. A year later, the Ohio State Bar Association adopted the same code. To ensure that all Ohio lawyers were aware of these new requirements, extra copies of the proceedings of the 1909 annual meeting, including the canons, were printed, bound in paperback, and distributed to every member of the Ohio bar.

Words and deeds

Lawyers are often known for their love of words. Thus, it might be surprising that the first formal debate at an Association meeting was not held until 1904. The topic was whether municipalities should own utilities. Not wishing to be left out, at the 1909 meeting, the lawyers' spouses participated in a mock trial. Sadly, there is no record of who won what.

Membership continued to grow during the 1900s, albeit not as quickly as some members would have liked. The Hon. Peter A. Laubie, Salem, did not mince words in his annual address at Put-in-Bay during the summer of 1900. By that time, there were thousands of lawyers in Ohio, but fewer than 500 belonged to the Association. One of the reasons for this was popularly termed the

"Cuyahoga Complaint." At that time, many Cleveland lawyers did not think the Association addressed issues of concern to them.

Laubie noted in his address that although the Association had been organized in Cleveland 20 years earlier and held its annual meetings just three hours away (by "good transportation"), there were only six lawyer members from Cleveland—and even fewer Cleveland judges—present at the annual meeting. Considering that there were nearly 800 lawyers practicing in Cleveland at the time, he urged attorneys in Cleveland and elsewhere to become active in both their local and state bar associations.

Cleveland, as well as other major cities, would respond to his requests in later years. By 1909, there were 844 members, an all-time high. Perhaps because there were so many members, transportation to Put-in-Bay likely became an issue, and the summer meeting moved in 1910 to Cedar Point. The total cost of the 1909 annual meeting was $103.50.

During the first decade of the 20th century, two important members joined the Association. They were George W. Rightmire, future president of The Ohio State University, and George W. Ritter, Sandusky (who later moved to Toledo). Ritter drafted the plan to develop the Ohio Legal Center, the longtime home of the Association on the campus of The Ohio State University, and it was his gift in 1959 that allowed the building to be built on that site. This was the home of the Association until 1991.

chapter 6

War and More

Allen Andrews, Hamilton, OSBA president, 1910.

CEDAR POINT IN SANDUSKY, WHAT IN LATER YEARS would be known as "Ohio's Roller Coast," became the new site of the Association's annual summer meeting. The Breakers Hotel provided breezes from Lake Erie and a welcome break from the stuffy offices the lawyers occupied most of the year.

New members in 1910 included Frank B. Willis, a future Ohio governor and then U.S. senator, who ran unsuccessfully for president in 1928. George W. Ritter, one of the most significant figures in Association history, had left the organization for a few years but began to take a more active role in 1917.

Ritter's first reported concern was that there was little cooperation between the Association and local bar associations, and he suggested this issue be studied. That same year, the American Bar Association invited the Ohio State Bar Association president to come to a meeting of bar leaders in Philadelphia to discuss the same thing. N.B. Billingsley, Liston, was appointed to represent the Association at that meeting.

On staff

The first discussion of another important change, a paid staff for the Association, took place in 1919. The Association's secretary suggested that he be replaced with a full-time, paid secretary who could devote time to membership recruitment.

Membership in the Association in the early years showed advances and declines. By 1909, there were 842 members. The year 1912 marked the first time there were more than 1,000 members, and 319 came from Cleveland. So much for the "Cuyahoga Complaint"! The following year, Cincinnati added 143 new members. Numbers shifted through the rest of the decade, from 1,137 in 1914 back down to 1,089 in 1919.

Another key staff position was first suggested in the same year (1919) when President Ensign N. Brown argued that the

Clerks serving the Supreme Court of Ohio in 1911–1920: (left to right) Seba L. Miller, deputy clerk; Frank E. McKean, clerk; and Clinton Collins, deputy clerk.

Association must have a qualified representative in Columbus when the legislature was in session.

A woman who knew her place

Florence Ellinwood Allen took her place in Association history in 1912, when she became the first woman to speak at an annual meeting. She entered Western Reserve University in Cleveland at age 16, but women on that campus were not permitted to attend the schools of medicine or law at the time. Instead, she went to the University of Chicago, then to New York University Law School and graduated second in her class in 1913.

She was admitted to the Ohio bar in 1915 and went on to become the first female to serve on the Cuyahoga County Common Pleas Court, the Supreme Court of Ohio, and the U.S. Circuit Court of Appeals.

In 1991, Supreme Court of Ohio Justice Alice Robie Resnick wrote in *Ohio Lawyer* that she believed Judge Allen "would have been a U.S. Supreme Court justice had it not been for her gender."

The topic of Judge Allen's speech in 1912—and on a regular basis until 1920—was women's suffrage. The Ohio constitutional amendment to permit women to vote failed at the constitutional convention later that same year. It lost by more than 87,000 votes of a total of 586,000-plus cast on the issue.

Nevertheless, when the Women's Suffrage Party of Cuyahoga County approached Allen to run for justice of the Supreme Court of Ohio in 1920, she agreed—and became the first woman elected

LEFT: In 1912, Florence E. Allen became the first woman to speak at an annual Association meeting. She was admitted to the bar in 1915 and went on to become the first female to serve on the Cuyahoga County Common Pleas Court, the Supreme Court of Ohio, and the U.S. Circuit Court of Appeals. She is shown in her Supreme Court chambers in the '20s.

BELOW: Women's suffrage was a key issue at the 1912 Ohio Constitutional Convention. Shown here is a marker commemorating Union Chapel, also known as the "Free Speech" Chapel, in South Newbury, Geauga County, Ohio. Civil rights and suffrage speeches were given there by speakers including Susan B. Anthony, Lucy Stone, and Louisa May Alcott. The photograph is from the 1940s.

(*Ohio Historical Society*)

SUFFRAGETTE PARADE 7 30 14

OPPOSITE: Postcards, placards, and other printed materials supported women's right to vote. Shown is a 1915 postcard sent from Columbus to Athens with the slogan, "Let Ohio Women Vote."

ABOVE: The Association heard much discussion about women's right to vote. Shown is a parade of suffragettes campaigning for the vote in Columbus on July 30, 1914. Ohio ratified the 19th Amendment, extending suffrage to women, on June 16, 1919.

(*Ohio Historical Society*)

justice in the United States. She served on the Supreme Court of Ohio for two terms, then was appointed to the U.S. Court of Appeals for the Sixth Circuit, serving for 25 years until her retirement in 1959. Though her name was first proposed for the U.S. Supreme Court in 1934, she was never nominated, and she died in the mid-'60s.

Ohio constitutional issues

It is not particularly surprising to note that attorneys from throughout the state made numerous suggestions to the Association regarding what should be covered at a state constitutional convention. Besides the discussion of women's suffrage, key suggestions were:

- The governor, with the advice and consent of the Senate, should appoint the justices of the Supreme Court of Ohio;
- Adoption of the initiative and referendum style of government (under which voters can initiate laws by petition and have them upheld or struck down by a statewide referendum);

- One or more common pleas courts in each county;
- Nonpartisan ballots be provided for the election of judges;
- An uneven number of justices on the Supreme Court of Ohio; and
- All judges be lawyers and reside in the district or county from which they were elected.

There were 119 delegates to the Ohio Constitutional Convention, including 45 lawyers. Fifteen of those were members of the Ohio State Bar Association. The convention approved 11 of the proposals the Association first suggested, and 10 passed by the vote of the people.

Introductions are in order

The decade between 1900 and 1919 was perhaps the first time that Association members had admitted to themselves that they wanted their annual meetings to be more than just a scholarly exchange of views and a laundry list of suggestions.

A reception committee was first appointed in 1915. The Association president, the Hon. John N. Van Deman, Dayton, noted that one of the Association's objectives was to cultivate social relations among the members of the bar. The committee

was to ensure that all annual meeting attendees, as well as their spouses and children, would be introduced to each other and to the members.

These introductions were an indirect way to promote future annual meeting attendance. The philosophy was that if spouses and children were encouraged to make acquaintances, they would want to return to future annual meetings, and the lawyers would also return.

The Association had become increasingly involved with the issues of state government. To help members become more familiar with pending legislation, it instituted an annual midwinter meeting. The first one was held in December 1915 in Cincinnati.

Another first came a few months later at the 1916 summer convention, when two individuals vied for the Association presidency and two more for the job of secretary. History tells there were clear winners and no bitter battles.

Rumblings with a horrific consequence

Time travelers from the 21st century would be very familiar with a key item at the winter 1916 meeting. Attendees discussed basic conditions of national security—then as they related to World War I. A letter from the National Security League invited the bar to send three delegates to a January 1917 meeting in Washington, D.C., to consider security as well as the development of a strong national spirit.

In the summer of 1917, the Association sent a telegram to the president of the United States saying in effect that all members recognized that the country was confronting a "great crisis." The telegram also stated, on behalf of the members, "We do pledge ourselves to uphold and aid in every way to the full extent of our power the Nation and the president...."

The Association further supported the war effort by notifying local bar association secretaries that they should volunteer to handle the work of the members who had entered the armed services. Members also voted to make cash gifts to the American Red Cross and the YMCA to help those serving the country.

In summer 1918, the annual meeting was held in Cleveland. It was the first annual meeting to be held anywhere other than Put-in-Bay or Cedar Point since 1887. There were several reasons for the move: World War I had brought a somber mood to the country, and many families were making significant sacrifices; they had neither the will nor the resources to attend a resort-style meeting. Also, dozens of Association members were serving their

OPPOSITE: **There were 119 delegates to the 1912 Ohio Constitutional Convention, including 15 members of the Association. The opening of the convention at the Ohio Statehouse in Columbus on Jan. 9, 1912, is shown here.** (Ohio Historical Society)

country, as denoted by asterisks that accompanied the names of 57 members on the 1918 roster.

That same year, lawyers could attend both the Ohio State Bar Association's and the American Bar Association's annual meetings; both were in Cleveland simultaneously. Since the winter meeting had been canceled due to the war, the annual meeting agenda was more crowded, and more could be covered without required travel time to a resort. (The 40th annual meeting in 1919 marked a return to Cedar Point.)

During World War I, the anti-German feeling was pervasive. For example, when the Hon. John A. Schauck, Dayton (who had been elected president of the Association in July 1917), died before he could preside over the 1918 meeting, the Hon. Maurice H. Donahue felt compelled to note in his eulogy, "Although of German parentage, Schauck had no sympathy with Prussian militarism ... he expressed in the most vigorous language he could command his supreme contempt for that 'kultur'...."

The subject of dues resurfaced in 1918. Blame a war mentality, tough economic conditions throughout the state, or the fact that dues had remained the same for decades. Still, over strenuous objection, the dues more than doubled that year, from $2 to $5. At the same time, dues were waived for soldiers.

Raising the bar

The decade between 1910 and 1919 was also time to take another serious look at the requirements to become a member of the bar. In 1911, President Allen Andrews of Hamilton noted at the summer meeting that attitudes toward the law and lawyers, judges, and justices continued to be criticized and that this was giving rise to a general attitude of dissatisfaction with the law. To overcome this, he suggested, would require a better system of schools, colleges, churches, the press, the bench and the bar.

By 1915, changes were in the works. An approved Association report suggested that those admitted to the bar should undergo three years of legal study if they were graduates of the literary department of colleges or universities approved by the state Supreme Court, or four years if they were graduates in any other area. Second, only graduates of high school, college, universities or a school system with an equal grade would be permitted to take the bar exam. No high school equivalency exam would be accepted. Finally, every applicant would also be required to take a one-year ethics course.

OPPOSITE—

TOP: Ohioans celebrating the end of World War I in Columbus on Nov. 11, 1918. Dozens of members of the Association served during the war.

BOTTOM: On Nov. 11, 1919, Ohioans celebrated the first anniversary of Armistice Day on the grounds of the Statehouse in Columbus.

(Ohio Historical Society)

President Woodrow Wilson visits
Columbus on Dec. 10, 1915.
(*Ohio Historical Society*)

Ohio State Bar Association Report
on the horizon

What could be considered a precursor to the *Ohio State Bar Association Report* first appeared as a result of the 1919 Spidel Bill, which established a single publication covering Court of Appeals decisions, published by the office of the reporter of the Supreme Court of Ohio. The Association raised the price of each volume from $1.50 to $2.50. This was the beginning of the end for all the previous independent publications that offered only a few judicial decisions from a few jurisdictions.

John L.W. Henney was elected the first executive director of the Association in July 1920. Earlier the same year, he had been appointed reporter of the Supreme Court of Ohio (he had been an assistant in the office since 1903). His dual responsibilities led to a significant publication four years later, discussed in the next chapter.

chapter 7

How the '20s Roared

Association member Harry M. Daugherty spoke at the annual convention of the Association in 1921 when he was the U.S. attorney general. Daugherty, who was born in Fayette County in 1860, was instrumental in the election of Warren G. Harding as president and is shown at Harding's home during the 1920 presidential campaign. Though Harding was appreciative of his work, Daugherty was forced from office by President Calvin Coolidge in 1924. He was prosecuted for an alleged conspiracy to defraud the U.S. government, but the case was dismissed when two juries failed to agree. Daugherty returned to Ohio to practice law and died in 1941.

BELOW: John W. Bricker joined the Association in the 1920s. He served as Ohio governor from 1939-1945 and was one of numerous Association members who aspired to higher office. He is shown here campaigning for the office of vice president of the United States in 1944.

(Ohio Historical Society)

OHIO DOMINATED THE POLITICAL SCENE IN THE early 1920s. In 1921, Marion's Warren G. Harding was president of the United States; William Howard Taft, an ex-officio member of the Association, was chief justice of the United States; and Harry M. Daugherty of Washington Court House, another member, was the U.S. attorney general.

Taft and Daugherty as well as John W. Davis, who would be the Democratic candidate for president in 1924, spoke at the Association's annual meeting in Cincinnati in 1921.

Another person who would have national significance, Wendell L. Willkie, Akron, appeared on the Association's membership rolls for the first time in 1921 (though his initial membership record lists him as "Wardell").

Other key members who joined during this decade included John W. Bricker, a future attorney general, governor and U.S. senator; and Harold L. Bevis of Cincinnati, who would go on to be a member of the Supreme Court of Ohio and president of The Ohio State University.

The '20s are also significant in Association history because in 1929 the Association celebrated its 50th anniversary with membership at a record 3,600-plus. At that time, there were 31 standing and special committees.

A decade of firsts

The Association made numerous positive moves in the '20s. In 1920, the Association found its first permanent home in the offices of Ballard, Price and Jones in the Hartman Building in Columbus. (The Hyatt on Capitol Square now occupies the space where the Hartman Building stood.) Rent was $20 per month. In 1923, the Association moved to permanent headquarters in the Statehouse in space the Supreme Court of Ohio provided.

The Association designated an executive secretary in 1921. Each year, this person kept an office in Columbus and traveled

RIGHT: Hartman Building, the Association's first permanent home in 1920.

OPPOSITE—

TOP: Friends Henry Ford, Thomas Edison and Harvey Firestone are pictured with President Warren G. Harding on a camping trip that the four took in Maryland with their families, July 23-24, 1921.

FAR LEFT: President Harding on the golf course in the 1920s.

LEFT: James M. Cox and Franklin Delano Roosevelt, Columbus, Ohio, ca. 1920. James Middleton Cox (March 31, 1870-July 15, 1957) was a governor of Ohio, U.S. representative from Ohio and the Democratic candidate for president of the United States in the election of 1920. His running mate was Franklin D. Roosevelt. Cox was defeated in the 1920 presidential election by fellow Ohioan Warren G. Harding.

(*Ohio Historical Society*)

throughout the state talking with individuals and small groups, urging them to join the Association. Harry F. Bell, who held the office in 1922, visited 37 cities and towns in the state in a single year.

The executive secretary was also responsible for creating bulletins to explain recent state legislation, to lobby members of the General Assembly on behalf of the Association, and to meet with legislative committees and the governor to explain particular positions. In 1923, Executive Secretary Robert D. Mason had developed such a strong network with the newspapers that more than 2,000 stories mentioning the Association appeared that year alone.

The Association hired a solicitor in 1927 with the sole purpose of increasing membership. He was paid $4 for each new member, $1.50 for a single year of delinquent dues, and $2.50 if dues were delinquent for more than one year. This was a wise move since it led to the addition of 147 new members in one year, and the old debts decreased significantly.

This decade also brought the Association's first real effort to attract younger lawyers. It sent letters to all applicants for admission to the bar prior to the bar exam, congratulating them on their career choice and urging them to study hard. At the admissions ceremony, members of the Supreme Court of Ohio as well as representatives of the state and local bar associations welcomed the new lawyers and explained why they should join the Ohio State Bar Association.

A plan to incorporate the Association took root in 1921, and a committee was appointed to help guide a plan for incorporation through the legislature.

1924 OSBA annual meeting.
(*Ohio Historical Society*)

THE OHIO STATE
BAR ASSOCIATION,
COLUMBUS, JAN. 25, 1924.

Columbus
Studio
109 1 N. High St.
Columbus, Ohio.

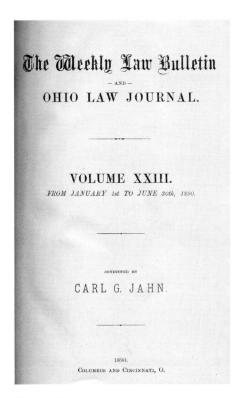

The *Weekly Law Bulletin*.

BELOW: In 1928, the *Weekly Bulletin* expanded to include more Association reports and full publication of the Supreme Court of Ohio and appellate opinions. Its name changed to the *Ohio State Bar Association Report*.

My Weekly Bulletin

The Association's first attempt to communicate with members on a weekly basis began in 1924 with the *Weekly Law Bulletin*, which held news of Supreme Court of Ohio cases, reports on the status of bills in the legislature, and other items of general interest. This was the work of John Henney, the combination secretary/ executive director and Supreme Court reporter. The *Bulletin* (a precursor to the *Ohio State Bar Association Report*) enjoyed quick popularity and received a large portion of the Association's first-ever budget in 1925: $5,000.

The *Bulletin* continued as an experimental publication until 1928, when it became a permanent benefit offered to all members. Henney was in charge of this weekly offering until his death in 1950. Because the member benefits included the successful *Bulletin*, dues were increased to $8 at the 1927 annual meeting.

On April 13, 1928, the *Bulletin* expanded to include more reports of activities of the state as well as local bar associations, proceedings of the Supreme Court of Ohio, and the full publication of the opinions of the Supreme Court of Ohio and the courts of appeal. The publication's name later changed to *Ohio State Bar Association Report* and included advertising, another key source of revenue for the Association. By 1929, the publication even included a regular review of newspaper comments about the Association and lawyers in general.

A new corporate code for Ohio

The Association did extensive work on a corporate code and submitted it to the state legislature in 1927. This code would update laws in place since 1846 and remained in place with few amendments until 1955, when one member of the original Corporation Code Committee, Paul K. Bickel, spearheaded its comprehensive revision.

In addition, the Association appointed 25 lawyers to draft and submit a set of canons of legal ethics that the Supreme Court of Ohio had requested.

As was true almost every other decade, there was much discussion regarding the standards and requirements for lawyers and legal practice. In 1920, George W. Rightmire, who was then chairman of the Committee on Legal Education, reported the results of the committee's study of the educational background of those admitted to the Ohio bar from 1907 to 1916. During that time, Rightmire reported, only 64 percent of those taking the bar exam had graduated from high school, and only 61 percent had graduated from a law school. The others had spent at least some time "reading the law," which constituted working in a law office in lieu of classroom training. In those 10 years, about 75 percent of would-be lawyers passed the bar exam.

Legal training revisited

Despite the Association's recommendations in 1915, no changes in the standards for admission to the practice of law had been made since 1900. In 1921, there was a strong argument that college training should be required for lawyers. A year later, there was a discussion with members of the Supreme Court of Ohio, during which Association members recommended that anyone studying law should attend at least two years of college first.

By 1929, the Association's Committee on Legal Education, through its member Arthur A. Miller, Cleveland, had proposed more training. His committee was considering requirements that included the completion of a standard four-year college course before admission to law school, as well as two exams relating to ethics, character, natural ability, education and motives for practicing law—one before any law study and another taken with the bar exam.

Interestingly, those who wished to attend law school in Ohio had more schools from which to choose in the 1920s than they do today. The law schools open in 1929 were John Marshall School of Law, Rufus P. Ranney Law School, Cleveland Law School, and Western Reserve University Law School, all in Cleveland; University of Cincinnati College of Law, Judge F.R. Gusweiler's, and a YMCA School, all in Cincinnati; Toledo University Law School and St. John's College in Toledo; The Ohio State University and a YMCA School in Columbus; Ohio Northern University at Ada, and a YMCA School in Youngstown. (YMCA law schools were developed as part of a nationwide program sponsored by the Association to make legal education affordable, practical and accessible.)

Many law students were thankful that a suggestion made in 1921 by then-Association President Daniel W. Iddings met with no success. He recommended that all law students be required to pass a test on the Bible and Shakespeare just to be eligible to take the bar exam. Later, he suggested a test on Blackstone's Commentaries as a must.

President Iddings also expressed concern about an issue that would cause much future discussion—lawyer advertising. "We should censor legal advertisements so as to keep our members

Ohio Law Schools

The law schools in Ohio are Capital University Law School, Columbus; Case Western Reserve University School of Law, Cleveland; Cleveland State University Cleveland-Marshall College of Law, Cleveland; Ohio Northern University Pettit College of Law, Ada; The Ohio State University Moritz College of Law, Columbus; University of Akron School of Law, Akron; University of Cincinnati College of Law, Cincinnati; University of Dayton School of Law, Dayton; and University of Toledo College of Law, Toledo.

CAPITAL UNIVERSITY
LAW SCHOOL

The law school was established in 1903 as part of a YMCA-sponsored national program. The plan was to make legal education affordable, practical and accessible. It affiliated with Capital University in 1966.

Capital University is the largest university in the country affiliated with the Evangelical Lutheran Church of America and was founded in 1830. Incorporated 20 years later, the university also offers joint degrees with other colleges and the law school. There are more than 30 faculty members and more than 1,000 students.

CASE WESTERN RESERVE UNIVERSITY
SCHOOL OF LAW

This Cleveland university was founded in 1892. It was one of the first schools accredited by the American Bar Association and was a charter member of the American Association of Law Schools. In 2004, there were 704 students, including 40.6 percent who were women, and more than 300 different undergraduate degrees were represented.

Since 1997, more than 130 new courses, including classes in bioethics and social work, have been added to the curriculum, and degree options include JD/MBA and JD/MS (biochemistry).

CLEVELAND STATE UNIVERSITY
CLEVELAND-MARSHALL
COLLEGE OF LAW

The law college is now 100 years old and was the first in the state to admit women. It was also among the first to admit minorities.

Its Academic Support programs strengthen the law school curriculum by paying special attention to the skills involved in developing the requirements necessary to succeed in law school. There are several special programs emphasizing academics.

Students who attend Cleveland State enjoy one-on-one assistance with several faculty members who can answer questions about curriculum and the analysis of exam answers.

The university also provides a six-week bar exam essay workshop eight weeks before the annual bar to ensure that students focus on analysis, style and form.

OHIO NORTHERN UNIVERSITY
PETTIT COLLEGE OF LAW

In Ada, this college began in 1885, and each year welcomes students from more than 150 undergraduate colleges and more than 30 states. The school is on a comfortable campus and prides itself in its small classes and personal attention to students. Students can also benefit from the fact that the faculty members are experienced practitioners and that there is a low student/faculty ratio.

THE OHIO STATE UNIVERSITY
MICHAEL E. MORITZ
COLLEGE OF LAW

The first classes of the Ohio State Law College began in 1891 in Franklin County Courthouse and included 32 students and one woman. The law school moved to Ohio State's Orton Hall in 1894 and was elevated to college status in 1896.

It moved to its first permanent home, Page Hall, in 1903 and to the current college in 1958, expanding in 1993. The school was named the Moritz College of Law in 2001 in recognition of the support of 1961 graduate Michael E. Moritz.

THE UNIVERSITY OF AKRON
SCHOOL OF LAW

The school was founded in 1921 and aims to provide legal education for working peo-ple and those who otherwise might not have the option to enter the legal profession. As a result, there is a significant focus on evening programs. The school focuses on scholarship—not just law review articles but also law reform and general writing that require research, analysis and original thought. The faculty strives for excellence in teaching and focuses on establishing an understanding of professionalism and high ethical standards.

The school actively participates with individuals, the courts, professional organizations and the government and also works with local, national and international communities.

UNIVERSITY OF CINCINNATI
COLLEGE OF LAW

The university is the fourth oldest continually operating law school in the country and has had a law school since 1833. In 1896, then-Dean William Howard Taft supervised the merger of the Cincinnati Law School with the University of Cincinnati, and it became the University's College of Law.

It is a founding member of the Association of American Law Schools. Its annual juris doctor program intentionally includes fewer than 400 students to create a solid student/ faculty ratio.

UNIVERSITY OF DAYTON
SCHOOL OF LAW

The University of Dayton School of Law is part of the University of Dayton, a Catholic Marianist University, and was established in 1922. It closed in 1935 during the Depression but reopened in 1974. It received provisional accreditation by the American Bar Association in 1974–1975 and full accreditation from the American Bar Association Council of the Section of Legal Education and Admissions to the Bar in 1979. It received membership in the Association of American Law Schools in 1984.

The state-of-the-art law building allows students to participate in a contemporary experience while they represent real clients under the supervision of law faculty. Students work with lawyers and judges in the Law Technology programs, which provide potential employment and assist students in other ways as well.

Students are encouraged to listen, to respect, to demonstrate compassion and to solve problems in a creative way while keeping an eye on ethics issues.

UNIVERSITY OF TOLEDO
COLLEGE OF LAW

The University of Toledo is near downtown Toledo, yet in a residential neighborhood. It offers more than 250 undergraduate and graduate academic programs. It has more than 20,000 students from throughout the world. It is especially proud of its $17.3 million student recreation center and its affiliation with the Toledo Museum of Art.

The university bills itself as "very affordable" with numerous scholarships. There are more than 500 students from more than 200 schools and universities across the country. There are four certificate programs that recognize advanced study, including environmental law, international law, intellectual property and technology law. Joint degrees, including a JD/MBA and a JD/ME, are also available.

from advertising their wares on the same plane as soap and farm lighting systems," he said. "This sort of advertising is certainly not respectful and is entirely out of keeping with the ancient traditions of our profession."

Choosing judges

Another concern of the '20s would resurface years later. At the 1923 midwinter meeting, there was much discussion regarding the nomination and election of judges. One member noted that the Supreme Court of Ohio ranked only 23rd in the country in the number of times its decisions were cited in briefs in other states. At the same time, high courts in Massachusetts, New York and Pennsylvania—where the judges were either appointed or elected for long terms—were cited more often than courts in states that held shorter-term judicial elections. Association members offered some unusual proposals for changing Ohio's selection of judges. These included leaving the selection of judges to lawyers, or penalizing judicial candidates for

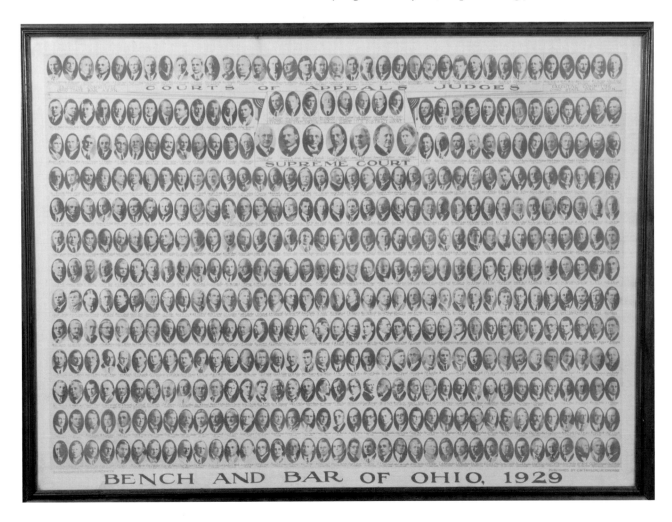

campaigning. No conclusions were reached, however, and the subject was eventually tabled, but in succeeding years this subject would occupy a great deal of the Association's time and effort.

Adding to the agenda

At the Association's 1920 winter meeting in Dayton, numerous special events were first added to the program. There were several luncheons and teas as well as a formal banquet, a dance, and a tour of Dayton and the surrounding areas. Also, a luncheon for alumni of the University of Cincinnati Law School was added to the annual meeting in 1927.

In 1929, the Association appointed a Women's Welfare Committee, whose achievements would include adding women to the probate courts' lists of appraisers and an appropriation of $35,000 for a vocational training school at the Marysville Reformatory.

chapter 8

Voices of the Depression

The steel frame of the State Office Building on Front Street in Columbus, May 1, 1931. The groundbreaking had taken place Nov. 19, 1929. The art deco building opened March 27, 1933, and was used for public assemblies and hearings, state offices, and the State Library of Ohio. On Feb. 17, 2004, the Supreme Court of Ohio relocated to the building and now uses it for the Supreme Court and its affiliated offices. (*Ohio Historical Society*)

WHILE THE DEPRESSION THAT HIT THE COUNTRY in the '30s had an effect on the Association, too, members rarely strayed from the tasks at hand. It did, however, shorten the 1933 annual meeting to one and a half days.

In 1932, the Association received national recognition from the American Bar Association. In the fifth anniversary publication of the *Ohio State Bar Association Report*, the ABA president noted that he visited Ohio to "see how to run" a state bar association. He also commended the Ohio State Bar Association for devoting more time and effort to the problems of the profession than any other state bar association.

That same year saw the founding of the National Conference of Bar Examiners. More praise for the Association: Two of the conference's significant objectives were almost identical to goals earlier set by the Association. Improving the standards of legal training and requiring thorough character investigations for each bar admission applicant were musts in Ohio—and now throughout the country.

Put it in writing

The Association developed more business sense during the '30s. In 1931, a new accounting system was put into place. It featured a membership record listing each lawyer by name, address, appellate district, date of admission to the bar and date of affiliation with the OSBA.

By 1934, the Association had its own law library at the Deshler-Wallick Hotel

THE DESHLER-WALLICK
"America's Most Beautifully Equipped Hotel"
COLUMBUS, OHIO
L. C. Wallick, Pres.

Deshler-Wallick Hotel.
(*Ohio Historical Society*)

in downtown Columbus. In 1936, it added an assistant secretary, and in 1939, the Association was so busy that it hired two assistants to help operate the office.

After months of debate, the Association made key amendments to its own constitution in 1936. One of these created the Council of Delegates, calling for the inclusion of at least two delegates from each Ohio county. If no local bar association or lawyers' club existed in a particular county, the lawyers of that county would meet to choose two delegates.

It was decided that district vice presidents and Executive Committee members would be elected by mail ballots, and the Association would publish names of all applicants for membership before they were admitted. Finally, the Association president was no longer required to make an opening address at the annual meeting, though he was still welcome to do so.

A call to young members

Membership focus turned to young lawyers. The Junior Bar began in 1934 and included those who had been members of the bar for eight years or less. Again, the American Bar Association was impressed with Ohio's initiative in this area, and when it began its own Junior Bar later that same year, it patterned its bylaws after Ohio's Junior Bar Code of Regulations. As a further incentive to join the Association, young lawyers were to pay dues of $4 rather than the regular rate of $8 during the first four years after their admission to the bar.

George Bellows and a Goodyear zeppelin

During the '30s, Association meetings continued to include much more than legal issues. The 1931 midwinter meeting in Columbus included a trip to the new Columbus Gallery of Fine Arts and a viewing of the works of Columbus native George Bellows. There was also a trip to the top of the city's tallest building, what is now the LeVeque Tower, and a special tea in nearby Bexley.

An Association-sponsored event at the 1933 winter meeting in Akron included a tour of the Goodyear Zeppelin Air Dock. (*Ohio Historical Society*)

Events at the 1933 winter meeting in Akron were more spectacular, including a tour of the Goodyear Zeppelin Air Dock to see the USS *Macon*, the nearly completed lighter-than-air warship. It was the world's biggest, and the dock where it was being constructed was the largest building without interior support. (The *Macon* flew only until February 1935, when it collapsed during a flight in California, killing two.)

Reflecting members' interest in flying, the Association had developed an Aviation Committee by 1934. Its first member was Clevelander Thomas J. Herbert, who had been an aviation ace during World War I and would later serve as state attorney general and governor.

In 1938, an amendment to the Association's constitution eliminated the winter and summer meetings to avoid snow and heat, and replaced them with meetings in April and October.

In 1939, Association members at the first fall meeting were invited to attend the Notre Dame-Navy football game at Cleveland Stadium as well as a theater party, a fashion show and a luncheon in Shaker Heights.

Preview of a presidential candidate

Former Association member Wendell Willkie was a key speaker at the 1933 winter meeting, seven years before the Republican party nominated him for president. A year later, at the 55th annual meeting, the Association heard from its only surviving charter member, the Hon. Edmund B. King of Sandusky. King died later that year at age 84.

Another prominent member during this time was Harold Burton, who served as a Cleveland mayor, a U.S. senator, and a U.S. Supreme Court justice. He was joined by fellow U.S. Sens. Robert J. Bulkley and Atlee Pomerene and U.S. Rep. Paul Howland.

Once more with feeling

Decade after decade, the Association continued to debate key issues such as lawyer training requirements, lawyer advertising and judicial selection.

While discussions about judicial qualifications and selection had begun in the '20s, it was in 1933 that the Association's Judicial Administration and Legal Reform Committee first suggested that judges be appointed with the consent and approval of a judicial nominating commission. This proposal was termed the "Ohio Plan" (and was later nationally known as the "Missouri Plan").

Past officers of the OSBA. This photo was taken at the last state bar meeting at Cedar Point in 1937. Pictured left to right: Charles W. Racine, Toledo, OSBA president 1935; Andrew S. Iddings, Dayton, OSBA president 1942; Donald A. Finkbeiner, Toledo, OSBA president 1940; Walter S. Ruff, Canton, OSBA president 1937; Chester G. Wise, Akron, OSBA president 1941; George R. Murray, Dayton, OSBA president 1936; J.L.W. Henney, OSBA secretary and first executive director; Gerritt J. Fredriks, Cincinnati, OSBA president 1939; unknown officer; Howard L. Barkdull, Cleveland, OSBA president 1938.

Two years later, the same committee suggested something similar, now known as the "Cleveland Plan." According to its provisions, the governor would appoint all the judges on the Court of Appeals and the Supreme Court of Ohio with the advice and consent of the Ohio Senate. A year later, the Association membership formalized and endorsed the plan.

For the first time in 1938, the Association decided to participate in a statewide campaign to amend the Ohio Constitution to include the "Cleveland Plan." Members of the Association barnstormed the state, speaking to clubs, community organizations, and other groups, attempting to convince newspapers to support the position.

It was an inauspicious political beginning for the Association. The amendment failed by a margin of 2 to 1 and lost in every county. That fall, the Association made a second effort with another round of speeches and stumping, but the amendment again lost in every county by nearly 2 to 1.

Another issue that was debated in the '30s also dealt with professional standards. The Junior Bar established a committee to investigate the unauthorized practice of law in 1935. This topic would be the subject of more discussion in future years.

U.S. Presidents from Ohio

James A. Garfield	(Orange)
Ulysses S. Grant	(Point Pleasant)
Warren G. Harding	(Corsica)
Benjamin Harrison	(North Bend)
William H. Harrison	(North Bend)
Rutherford B. Hayes	(Delaware)
William McKinley	(Niles)
William H. Taft	(Cincinnati)

LEFT: Ulysses S. Grant, born in Point Pleasant, Ohio, was U.S. president from 1869 to 1877.

ABOVE: President James A. Garfield from Orange served as the 20th president of the United States from March 4, 1881, to Sept. 9, 1881.

(Ohio Historical Society)

Fort Meigs Memorial, Perrysburg. William Henry Harrison built Fort Meigs on the Maumee River in 1813 to protect northwest Ohio and Indiana from British invasion. This photograph was taken ca. 1940-49. (Ohio Historical Society)

U.S. Supreme Court Justices from Ohio

The state has also contributed more than its share of U.S. Supreme Court justices. Ten have been from the Buckeye State. Between 1881 and 1887, and again between 1921 and 1922, three Ohioans were present on the Court. Ohio chief justices led the Court for 35 years, with three of the 16 chief justices from Ohio. The last was Potter Stewart, who retired in 1981. Supreme Court justices from Ohio are listed below.

NAME	PRESIDENT	YEARS	RESIDENCE
John McLean	Jackson	1829–1861	Lebanon/Cincinnati
Salmon P. Chase	Lincoln	1864–1873	Cincinnati
Morrison R. Waite	Grant	1874–1888	Maumee/Toledo
William B. Woods	Hayes	1880–1887	Newark
Stanley Matthews	Garfield	1881–1889	Cincinnati
William R. Day	Roosevelt	1903–1922	Canton
John H. Clarke	Wilson	1916–1922	Lisbon/Youngstown
William H. Taft	Harding	1921–1930	Cincinnati
Harold H. Burton	Truman	1945–1958	Cleveland
Potter Stewart	Eisenhower	1958–1981	Cincinnati

Strengthening the bar

While it had not prevailed in the matter of judicial selection, the Association was more successful in its attempt to change the requirements for admission to the bar. In 1933, representatives of the Association (along with the dean of The Ohio State University's College of Law and others) met with members of the Supreme Court of Ohio to recommend changes in admission requirements for the bar that would broaden the content of the bar exam, increase emphasis on applicants' backgrounds and ethical fitness, and include a stipulation that no applicant could take an exam more than three times.

About a year later, the Supreme Court of Ohio did adopt some of these changes. It revised the bar exam to include questions about municipal corporations, trusts and conflict of law. Committees were to interview prospective members of the bar regarding their character, reputation and moral fitness. Candidates also had to complete questionnaires that the Supreme Court of Ohio created.

In 1935, the Supreme Court of Ohio took another step that pleased the Association immensely. It announced that, after Sept. 1, no one could practice law simply by "reading law" in a law office. Instead, to be admitted to practice law in Ohio, an applicant would have to be a graduate of an ABA-approved law school, belonged to the League of Ohio Law Schools, or approved by the league.

A 1935 law, supported by the Association, also placed more emphasis on legal training. It required that all future probate court judges must be lawyers. This had been an Association discussion for about 50 years.

At the same time, the Association's attempt to require lawyers to be members did not meet with success. In fact, in 1939 the Cuyahoga County Bar Association took out an ad in the Association's publication opposing a mandatory association, calling it a "lawyers' union" and a "dictatorship."

Changes in Ohio law

The Association played an important part in changing other key provisions of Ohio law during the 1930s. In 1931, the legislature adopted a new probate code that Association members had created. Four years later, the Association was the author of the Appellate Procedure Act that the legislature passed, designed to simplify the method of appeal from a trial court's decision.

While the Association was trying to make changes to the law that would improve professional standards and streamline the operations of the courts, other legislation in the 1930s that did not receive the Association's attention included prohibitions on marathons, marathon dances, walkathons, talkathons, and skateathons.

chapter 9

Wartime Mentality and Recovery

WORLD WAR II APPEARED TO HAVE MUCH MORE impact on the Ohio State Bar Association than either World War I or the Depression. The first official mention of the conflict was at the 1941 spring meeting in Columbus, where a speaker explained Congress's 1940 Soldiers and Sailors Relief Act.

Members were urged to give free legal services to men who were serving their country and to provide no-cost advice regarding registration for the draft to any man of draft age. They also were asked to review all potential legal action to see if it might impact a member of the service or any dependents.

By 1945, more than 877 Ohio lawyers had been placed on active duty to serve their country in World War II. Shown are members of the 37th Infantry Division Color Guard marching up the steps of the Ohio Statehouse to turn over their flags at the conclusion of the war. (*Ohio Historical Society*)

Waymon B. McLeskey, Columbus,
OSBA president, 1943.

BELOW: Jay P. Taggart, Cleveland,
OSBA president, 1944.

Into the war

By summer 1942, 244 Ohio lawyers had been placed on active duty for their country. The number stood at 877-plus by early 1945. One, Maj. John C. Morley, returned to his practice after surviving the Bataan Death March in the Philippines; another, Capt. Paul W. Brown, Youngstown, was held as a prisoner of war in Italy. (After his return, he was elected to the Supreme Court of Ohio and then became state attorney general.)

Here at home, at least two lawyers worked nights at a war plant. Hot topics at Association meetings included "What Is the War Doing to Law and Lawyers?" and "Opportunities for Lawyers in the Army."

Law students who had entered the armed services before graduation were nonetheless permitted to take the bar exam—although their grades were withheld until the schools certified that they had completed their coursework. Nevertheless, only 14 women and 50 men took the June 1944 bar exam, compared with 400 who took it before the war.

Meetings during the war years were shortened or eliminated due to restrictions on travel and the federal government's request that hotel and train accommodations be kept available only for those directly involved in the war. The Association's Committee on the War Effort, which offered legal assistance to service members, kept busy and requested more help from members in 1945. Many responded and provided this free service.

War recovery efforts

The war's end brought more changes. The University of Cincinnati, The Ohio State University, and Toledo University offered free refresher courses for lawyers who had been in the service. Law book publishers offered discounts and some free books.

The number of would-be lawyers taking the bar exam rose again. In 1947, for example, 284 applicants passed the exam. One, Joseph B. Miller Jr. of Wapakoneta, joined the Association's staff the following year and later became its second executive director.

As part of the Association's postwar initiatives, it created a Legal Services Committee, which encouraged local bar associations to assist returning veterans. More than 6,000 individuals ultimately benefited from these advice programs. The Association also created a lawyer-veteran pamphlet to help address veterans' issues.

Redistricting, representation and other internal changes

After its years of war effort, in 1946 the Association focused on rewriting its constitution—the first complete rewrite since the document had been drafted in 1880. The revisions went into effect in 1947.

The new constitution abandoned appellate districts as the basis for Association representation, substituting instead 15 new state bar districts. It also provided for one annual meeting, increased the decision-making strength of the Council of Delegates, prohibited consecutive terms on the Executive Committee, allowed referendum votes on policy issues, and (perhaps to ensure a certain visibility for the president) once again required the chief officer to make an annual address.

Each Association district was entitled to one member on the Executive Committee and one or more members on the Council of Delegates (based on the lawyer population of the district). By June 1949, the system was comfortably in place, and there had been district meetings in 13 of the 15 districts.

The Association also resolved an internal issue regarding increased printing costs for the *Ohio State Bar Association Report* and the Supreme Court reports by changing printers. The Law Abstract Printing Co. in Norwalk took over the job from 1942 until 1968, when the Association purchased the company, later known as the Ohio Printing Co.

There was other good news in 1949 as the Association membership topped 6,000 for the first time. The staff had increased to four. Dues had been raised from $8 to $12, and income exceeded expenses by more than $14,000.

Meals and more

Meetings in the early and late '40s included amusing diversions. In 1941, the fall meeting was in Toledo, where the women lawyers, who had their own law club, invited all the female lawyers attending the meeting to a breakfast and an evening theater party. Political signs, music and songs highlighted the campaigns of the vice presidential election held in 1949, and the host committee entertained 300-plus spouses in what would become an integral part of future meetings.

Lunches for successful applicants to the bar began in 1947, scheduled in Columbus, Cincinnati and Cleveland following the induction ceremony. Was there such a thing as a free lunch? Perhaps not entirely. The Association and its Junior Bar Section were sponsors, and the new admittees were treated to a sales pitch about how the Association could help them and their future practice.

Another issue was resolved in spring 1940. After years of discussing the merits of requiring all Ohio lawyers to belong to the Association, a mandatory bar proposal was put to a vote. The members voted solidly against the concept, killing the idea for good.

Changes for the state

The Association saw its influence on the Ohio public increase during the decade in a number of ways. In 1940, a Columbus radio station had a regular show titled "Liberty under Law." The Association's Public Relations Committee worked with the station, developing the presentations and working with local bars to ensure that they were involved. Ultimately, 12 stations throughout the state aired the series.

The probate code was revised again in 1941, based on suggestions from the Association. Also, two Ohio constitutional amendments that the Association proposed became law in 1944. One authorized the Supreme Court of Ohio's chief justice, or the senior judge, to fill any vacancy on the Supreme Court of Ohio on a temporary basis with a judge from the court of appeals. The other allowed the legislature to set qualifications for judges, permitted the chief justice to assign appellate judges to sit in other jurisdictions, and covered other procedural issues.

In 1947, six of the 12 bills backed by the Association became law—perhaps in part because the reporter for the Association was now the acting majority leader in the Ohio Senate. Two years later, the tally was six of 11, including a Uniform Partnership Act, the Uniform Foreign Depositions Act, and some amendments to the probate and corporation codes.

In September 1950, the Association received special recognition from the American Bar Association and was chosen for an Award of Merit. Eight state bar associations had competed, and Ohio was chosen based on its accomplishments of the previous year as well as its novel ideas, wide variety of activities and success rate.

Though many may think of political action committees as a recent concept, PACs have been active for decades. Shown are members of the political action committee of the Ohio AFL-CIO discussing the Taft-Hartley Act in 1948 in Hamilton County, Ohio.
(*Ohio Historical Society*)

chapter 10

Into the Jet Age

Joe Miller, OSBA executive director from 1950 to 1986.

THERE WAS EVIDENCE IN THE 1950 PUBLIC RELATIONS Committee report to the Association that a new communication age had arrived. The report suggested for the first time that television might be used to convey lawyers' message to the public. This was just the first of many changes brought by the Jet Age.

Joseph B. Miller Jr., Wapakoneta, took over at the organization's helm. Miller had worked with John Henney, the first executive director, for two years and assumed the role when Henney died July 1, 1950.

Miller had served for three years in the Army Air Corps during and after World War II and in 1946 enrolled at the University of Michigan Law School. He had intended to practice law, he recalled in an *Ohio State Bar Association Report* interview in 1986, but learned of the position at the Association. He decided that the job could offer him "wider experience for law practice at a later date." That date, of course, never came.

Before stepping up as executive director, Miller served as the Association's lobbyist at the Statehouse for many years. He is also remembered for designing the Association logo used from 1955 to 1986, a torch and the seal of the Association with its name and the date 1880.

The tenor of America's political climate dictated another topic in 1953. The Council of Delegates considered whether communists should be permitted to be members—and voted conclusively to keep them out of the Association. At the same time, it did note that a lawyer had the right to defend anyone regardless of the cause involved.

The Association at 75

During the early '50s, the Association spent a great deal of time deciding how its 75th anniversary would be celebrated and on its plans to move to its own new building.

The 1955 celebration was in Dayton. Gov. Frank J. Lausche designated May 19, 1955, as "Ohio State Bar Association Day." A special 32-page program contained pictures of past members and a history of the Association. Attorneys who had practiced for 50 years or more received awards, and a brief history of the organization was published in the *American Bar Journal*.

The Association's 1954–1955 president, John C. Durfey, Springfield, expressed pride in the group's accomplishments, including the fact that it had grown to 8,000-plus members. He added that the burgeoning Association was short-staffed and needed to consider moving from the Statehouse Annex to a new home. A few months later, a subcommittee with Earl F. Morris in charge began to study construction of a new headquarters.

Finances were also in focus in the mid-'50s. In 1956, the Association decided to charge a fee to attend the annual meeting. The registration fee was $5—paid with little comment by that year's 1,150-plus attendees. That same year, dues were raised from $16 to $25, and two new districts were added to ensure more attorney representation on the Executive Committee and the Council of Delegates.

*Establishment of new organizations
and benefits*

In 1951, the Ohio State Bar Foundation was organized to promote research in the law, advance legal knowledge and improve the administration of justice. Van Aken, writing in *Buckeye Barristers*, noted that this was "one of the most successful ventures in the history of the Bar Association."

In 1953, a committee of the Ohio State Bar Foundation recommended filing the articles of incorporation to establish the Ohio Bar Title Insurance Co. The announcement came in a full-page ad in the *Ohio State Bar Association Report*.

It received its business license on April 15, 1955. The company's common stock was held by the Foundation and the preferred stock by about 900 lawyers. By 1958, it had issued more than 9,100 title policies with a face value of more than $131 million.

The Association announced this new benefit for its members during the '50s. It offered a group disability insurance plan to members in 1951, and seven years later it was followed by a group life insurance program. The latter proved especially popular, with more than 1,800 lawyers and their employers entering the program.

Ben C. Boer, Cleveland, OSBA president, 1951.

The Articles of Incorporation of

THE OHIO BAR
TITLE INSURANCE COMPANY

were filed July 23, 1953, by

a committee appointed by

THE OHIO STATE

BAR ASSOCIATION FOUNDATION,

which owns all of the common stock.

Subscriptions for preferred shares, to be sold at
$165 per share and which pay $7.50 per share dividends,
cumulative after two years, are now being received.

The Company will commence doing business after
the statutory capital of $100,000 and surplus of $50,000
have been paid in and approval has been granted by
the Division of Insurance.

For further information, consult the president or
secretary of your local bar association or communicate
with

Mac Lee Henney,
Trustee for The Ohio Bar
Title Insurance Company
8 East Broad Street
Columbus 15, Ohio
MAin 6565

The announcement of the Ohio Bar Title Insurance Company was featured as a full-page ad in a 1953 *OSBA Report*.

A signal of something to come also occurred in 1958 when the Executive Committee approved a plan allowing the Association to offer a professional liability insurance policy. The policy was underwritten by Seibert-Keck Insurance Agency Inc. and could be purchased for a three-year term.

By the end of the '50s, the Association was also seeing more increases in its staff, from six in 1953 to 10 in 1959.

A new home

A key move for the Association came in 1958 when it decided to construct a new headquarters on the campus of The Ohio State University next to the College of Law, at 33 W. 11th Ave. At one point, there was even talk of adding nearby buildings for the Supreme Court of Ohio and the Ohio Attorney General's Office, making it a true legal center, but that part of the plan was eventually dropped.

Funds for the building were to come from the Ohio State Bar Foundation, while the university would supply the land, build the building, and maintain and service it.

The building was estimated to cost $600,000. A goal was established for each county for the Association's first capital fund drive. Money came slowly but steadily, with more than $330,000 gathered by the time of the annual meeting in May 1959. Finally, George W. Ritter, Toledo, who had conceived the idea of the new building years earlier, promised that if the other members would raise a total of $450,000, he himself would contribute the final $150,000.

It was a good thing, since at the beginning of 1959, only 31 percent of the individual members of the Association had contributed. With continued effort throughout the rest of the year, essentially all the money was in place.

Publications and more

As the Association evolved, it worked on increasing its visibility across the state. In 1952, Harry S. Wonnell, Hamilton, published a president's message in the *Ohio State Bar Association Report* on the state of the Association. This practice was to continue on a regular basis for years to come.

■ LEADERSHIP
■ OPPORTUNITIES
■ LEARNING
■ REQUIREMENTS
■ FINANCIAL REWARD
■ PREPARATION

Planning Your Career in the Legal Profession

An example of publications the OSBA made for the public in the 1960s.
(*Ohio Historical Society*)

OPPOSITE: **The original *Ohio Lawyer* was launched in 1956.**

In 1955, the Public Relations Committee developed a series of pamphlets for the public on topics such as wills, home buying, marriage and the like. Churches, civic groups and local bar associations especially found these pamphlets useful. In 1956, the committee added another 14-page booklet on jury service and, later, one on installment buying. By 1957, it had distributed more than 2.2 million pamphlets.

Also in 1956, a publication called *Ohio Lawyer* was launched in an attempt to improve communication between the Association and the local bar associations. It did not work as well as hoped, and publication ended, though the name would later reemerge as the regular magazine for bar members.

In addition, the American Citizenship Committee launched a "Get Out the Vote" campaign, and the Junior Bar published a practice and procedure handbook.

A new code

In 1956, the Association again exercised its political muscle as it engineered the adoption of what was then known as Rule 27, allowing the Supreme Court of Ohio to have exclusive jurisdiction over lawyer discipline. This was especially important to members of the Association. Prior to the adoption of the rule, attorneys were disciplined by the county common pleas courts—sometimes leading to 88 or more different standards of conduct, as determined by each judge on each court. Rule 27 moved Ohio to the forefront regarding effective lawyer discipline by the states.

The biggest impact the Association had on Ohio law in the '50s came in 1953, when nine of the 13 measures it suggested became law. The most significant was H.B. 1, a complete revision of the Ohio Revised Code. The largest bill in Ohio history, it contained 6,870 pages and more than 6 million words. When there was concern in the Statehouse about the cost alone to print the final draft, the Association stepped in and helped secure an appropriation to cover printing expenses.

Sen. Carl D. Sheppard, in a letter to the Association, praised its involvement. "I feel it my duty as chairman of the Senate Judiciary Committee ... to say, in my judgment, your Association

Vol. 2, No. 5   THE OHIO LAWYER   May, 1962

Don't Miss The 1962 Annual Meeting

Outstanding Educational Institutes Set; Entertainment Features Touch All Corners

TOLEDO — An outstanding educational and social program will highlight the 82nd Annual Meeting of the Ohio State Bar Association, scheduled for May 10, 11 and 12 in Toledo. The headquarters hotel is the Commodore Perry.

Main speakers include A. Gilmore Flues, former assistant Secretary of the Treasury under the administration of President Dwight D. Eisenhower. The Washington, D.C., resident will

SYLVESTER C. SMITH is general counsel of The Prudential Insurance Co. of America, a position he has held since 1948. The American Bar Association president-elect received his law degree from New York Law School, New York, N. Y., in 1918. Prior to his affiliation with Prudential he practiced with his father in Phillipsburg, N. J. He is a past president of the New Jersey State Bar Association and the Association of Life Insurance Counsel.

(Photo by Bamberger Studios)

speak on "The Narcotic Problem—National and International" at the opening noon luncheon of the Convention, slated for May 10.

The annual banquet has obtained Sylvester C. Smith Jr., president-elect of the American Bar Association and general counsel for Prudential Insurance Company of America. The Newark, N. J., resident will speak

on "The Image of the Lawyer". The annual banquet will be held the evening of May 11.

Convention registration officially opens at 9 a.m. on May 10 and runs until 9 p.m. It will re-open all day on May 11 during the same hours. Payment of the $7 registration fee entitles registrants to admission to all institutes, educational sessions and certain social functions. There is an additional $5 fee for accompanying spouses.

In addition to hearing Flues at the May 10 luncheon, there will be nominations for State Bar vice president and recognition of Toledo Bar Association Annual Meeting committee chairmen for their fine efforts in staging the Convention.

The morning of May 10 will be devoted to the semi-annual

meeting of the Council of Delegates. The Thursday afternoon educational program includes a personal injury negligence institute concerned with "Medico-Legal Problems" and a securities institute on "Securities Pertaining to Small Corporations— Less than $300,000."

From 4 until 6 p.m., Mr. and Mrs. George W. Ritter will host the entire Convention at a reception and cocktail party at their magnificent Ottawa Hills estate.

The annual Local Bar Activities banquet is planned for 6:30 p.m. with Sherlock H. Evans, Massillon, acting as toastmaster. The guest speaker will be Richard M. Schmidt Jr., Denver, Colorado. His topic is entitled "The Language of Lawyers". In addition, outstanding Ohio local bar associations will be presented "Awards of Merit" for the development of novel programs aimed at improving the administration of justice and public understanding of the profession.

Thursday activities will conclude with a dance and show produced and staged by Toledo Bar members. It will be followed with a dance.

RITTER ESTATE—Pictured above is the estate of Mr. and Mrs. George W. Ritter, Ottawa Hills, a suburb of Toledo, site of the 82nd Annual Meeting of the Ohio State Bar Association, scheduled for May 10, 11 and 12. The Ritter mansion and garden will be the site of the May 10, 4 until 6 p.m., reception and cocktail party to be hosted by the Ritters for all Convention attendees.

(Photo by Lew Powers)

Friday functions commence at 9:30 a.m. with three institutes. They include antitrust, unauthorized practice of law and labor law. There also will be a program on "Judicial Selection, Past, Present and Future." Guest speaker will be Glenn R. Winters, executive director of the American Judicature Society, Chicago, Illinois.

State Bar President John C. Johnston Jr., Wooster, will deliver the annual President's address at the Friday noon luncheon, which will include a business meeting and voting on the proposed amendment to the OSBA Constitution.

Institutes scheduled for the afternoon of May 11 are real property; a Junior Bar Section program on "Economics and Office Management — The Art of Earning Money Gracefully"; professional corporations, and workmen's compensation.

The annual cocktail party takes place from 5:30 until 7 p.m. to be followed by the annual banquet. A dance, with music to be furnished by the Jimmy Dorsey band, Lee Castle conducting, will conclude Friday activities.

Two institutes are slated for Saturday morning. They are probate and trust law and criminal law. A complimentary brunch at 11 a.m. will end the 82nd Annual Meeting. Two breakfasts are scheduled for 8 a.m. on May 11. They are Ohio State Bar Association Foundation and Ohio State Law Alumni.

Other associations conducting concurrent meetings during the State Bar's Annual Meeting are Common Pleas Judges Association of Ohio, Ohio Judicial Conference, Ohio Association of Law Libraries, Municipal Judges Association of Ohio, Association of Ohio County Court Judges, The Ohio Association of Probate Court Judges, League of Ohio Law Schools and Prosecuting Attorneys' Association of Ohio.

The Ohio State Bar Association received top honors in the American Bar Association Award of Merit competition in 1953 for its work on the enactment of the Ohio Revised Code. President C. Kenneth Clark, Youngstown, and Secretary-Treasurer Joseph B. Miller are pictured here receiving the award from an ABA representative.

BELOW: President Dwight D. Eisenhower invited Ohio Governor Michael DiSalle and other state governors attending a national conference of governors to visit his farm in Gettysburg, Pa., in July 1962. DiSalle is pictured with New York Gov. Nelson Rockefeller, California Gov. Edmund G. "Pat" Brown and Eisenhower. (*Ohio Historical Society*)

saved the code from almost certain defeat.... You convinced the public and many senators that the Code was a worthy embodiment of the rules of community living in the middle of the 20th century." This work of the Association garnered it another Award of Merit from the American Bar Association.

More legislation

In 1954, the Association helped steer corporate code amendments through the legislature, resulting in a new non-profit corporation law for the state. During the same session, the Association was finally able to do something about what it felt were woefully inadequate salaries for Ohio judges, passing two separate bills to increase judicial wages.

Judicial retirement benefits were covered under a public employees retirement system bill. Also, the chief justice of the Supreme Court of Ohio was finally provided with an assistant, who could receive up to $10,100 in salary and travel expenses.

Annual Association meetings continued to offer elements of interest. In 1952, attendees at a summer institute at Denison University in Granville slept in dorm rooms and ate in the university's dining hall. A 1952 district meeting in Lancaster offered "Beauty Hints for Our Profession." In Akron in 1958, there was a simulated personal injury trial and a performance by a minister who doubled as a magician, as well as a speech by the president of the American Bar Association.

chapter 11

Home Sweet Home

TELEVISION MAY NOT HAVE MEANT MUCH TO THE members of the Association in 1950, but by 1960 it was a completely different story. The Convention Planning Committee was having a tough time landing a big-name speaker for the banquet. Months passed. Registration was slow. Finally, someone suggested Raymond Burr, the star of TV's hit "Perry Mason." (Shades of "I'm not a lawyer, but I play one on TV....") Burr agreed to speak, and suddenly registrations soared.

The resulting crowd of 1,000-plus filled a Cleveland ballroom and an adjoining dining room, and no one seemed to care that Burr's legal credentials were courtesy of Hollywood writers.

Television, radio and newspapers would again be the focus of a meeting—but in a much more negative light—just five years later in relation to the notorious Sam Sheppard murder trial in Cuyahoga County. Sheppard was accused of murdering his wife, and eventually there was so much pretrial publicity that a federal district court judge ordered Sheppard be released. (Sheppard's description of the killer was widely thought to be the inspiration for the elusive criminal in "The Fugitive," another '60s TV mystery show.)

Of backhoes and blacktop

The most lasting impact of the '60s, though, was the construction of the Ohio Legal Center. For decades, the Association staff were cramped in the tiny space in the Supreme Court Annex, but finally ground was broken on Sept. 10, 1960, and the agreement for the funding of the center involved The Ohio State University, the Ohio State Bar Foundation and the Association. On Oct. 28, 1961, three months ahead of schedule, the staff moved into the new Legal Center, 33 W. 11th Ave., Columbus. The building, which still stands, has three floors and a basement and had flowering trees and a reflecting pool in a formal

Law Day USA

School students from throughout Ohio compete each year in the "There Ought to Be a Law" contest. Students actually suggest what laws they think should be passed, and must explain why.

An annual luncheon for the winners is generally part of the annual Law Day—now Law Week—celebration.

Law Day was established in 1958 through the work of former American Bar Association President Charles S. Rhyne of Washington, D.C. He had seen the coverage media provided for the former Soviet Union's May 1 celebrations. "I was distressed that so much attention was given to war-making rather than peace-keeping," he recalled in a 2000 American Bar Association speech.

He put together a proclamation for President Dwight D. Eisenhower to sign, denoting May 1 as Law Day. He recalled that Eisenhower said at the time that the proclamation "praises our constitutional system of govern-ment, our great heritage under the rule of law and asks our people to stand up and praise what they have created."

In 1961, the U.S. Congress passed a resolution establishing Law Day as May 1 of every year "as a special day of celebration by the American people in appreciation of their liberties and reaffirmation of their loyalty to the United States of America...."

Since that time, Law Day has regularly been expanded to Law Week. The Association uses this time to remind the media, and the public, of just what the Association, and lawyers in general, can offer to them.

The student program is key because "[It] helps high school students prepare for citizenship as adults," said former Association President Stephen E. Chappelear of Columbus. "They come to understand first-hand the complex business of lawmaking."

garden. One of the blocks in the entrance wall was pulled from the wreckage of Gray's Inn in London after World War II.

The lobby and the reception area were on the first floor, which also housed the George W. Ritter Library, a board room, a conference room and office, kitchen and other support areas. The second floor housed the Association offices and equipment rooms, including a fully furnished president's office. The third floor housed the Ohio Legal Center Institute and the Ohio State Bar Foundation.

The Legal Center's formal dedication was June 22, 1962. Ritter, then 75, offered the dedication. Though nearly retired, Ritter spoke about current issues facing the Association at that time, including continuing legal education and scenarios to eliminate delays in court proceedings. His involvement with the Association, both in relation to the building and in terms of his other contributions, led to his receiving the Association's Ohio Bar Medal in 1967.

It is difficult to say if the future of the Association was affected more by its move to its own building or by a tool suggested by an Association president in 1965.

Before taking the Association reins, James F. Preston Jr. had been studying computerized legal data retrieval as part of his work with a bar committee for several years. As president, he began to work with the Mead Corp. on a program involving computer-based legal research.

The program began with a database containing only the Ohio Constitution, statutes and reported cases in Ohio. Mead established Mead Data Central to manage the operation, while the Association created the non-profit Ohio Bar Automated Research Corp. (OBAR) to sponsor it. In 1967, OBAR added its first full-time staff member to organize the research work and assist attorneys in the use of the system.

Years later, the Association gave the OBAR process to Mead, Mead continued its development, and today, the descendant of that program is known by researchers everywhere as LEXIS/NEXIS.

The Ohio Legal Center Institute and more

The 1960s were a decade of firsts, as the Ohio Legal Center Institute (later known as the Ohio Continuing Legal Education Institute, and now as the Ohio State Bar Association Continuing Legal Education Institute) came into being on July 17, 1961. This non-profit organization joined the academic community and the legal profession "to improve the administration of justice."

Another example of public education publications the OSBA distributed in the 1960s.
(*Ohio Historical Society*)

Ohio Bar Medal Award Winners

Ohio Bar Medal winner Denis J. Murphy receives his award from OSBA President H. Ritchey Hollenbaugh in 1993.

BELOW: Judge William K. Thomas (left) and John M. Adams (right) stand with 1993-94 OSBA President Kathleen B. Burke.

Albert L. Bell received the medal in 1996. He is pictured here with Jean, his wife.

BELOW: Frederick L. Oremus (right) is honored with the Ohio Bar Medal in 2001.

The Ohio Bar Medal Award is the Association's highest honor, and is awarded each year to an individual who exemplifies unusually meritorious service to the legal profession, to the community and to humanity.

1966 Judge Roy J. Gillen, Jackson
    Robert P. Goldman, Cincinnati
    Edwin L. Mitchell, Marion

1967 Judge Fred B. Cramer, Hamilton
    Carl D. Friebolin, Cleveland
    Alfred A. Benesch, Cleveland

1968 George W. Ritter, Toledo
    Louis J. Hofstadter, Hamilton

1969 Earl F. Morris, Columbus
    Francis L. Dale, Cincinnati
    Lisle M. Buckingham, Akron

1970 James F Preston Jr., Cleveland
    Richard F. Sater, Columbus
    Fred A. Smith, Toledo

1971 Chief Justice C. William O'Neill, Columbus

1972 C. Kenneth Clark Sr.,Youngstown
    Sol Morton Isaac, Columbus
    Judge Thomas M. Powers, Akron

1973 Bitner Browne, Springfield

1974 Samuel T. Gaines, Cleveland   James Olds Sr., Akron

1975 A. P. Feldman, Akron
    Wm. R. Van Aken, Cleveland
    C. Robert Beirne, Cincinnati

1976 Myron W. Ulrich, Cleveland

1977 Hon. Leonard J. Stern, Columbus

1978 Robert D. Moss, Barberton
    Merritt W. Green, Toledo

1979 J. Paul McNamara, Columbus   John A. Eckler, Columbus

1980 Joseph B. Miller, Columbus

1981 William B. Saxbe, Columbus
    Jamille G. Jamra, Toledo

1982 Paul C. Weick, Akron
    J. J. P. Corrigan, Cleveland (posthumously)

1983 William L. Howland, Portsmouth
    Richard M. Markus, Cleveland
    Franklin A. Polk, Cleveland
    John C. Elam, Columbus

1984 John V. Corrigan, Cleveland

1985 Honorable Robert M. Duncan, Columbus

1986 Honorable George Tyack, Columbus

1987 Justice Robert E. Holmes, Columbus

1988 Jack R. Alton, Columbus
    William W. Milligan, Columbus
    Bruce I. Petrie, Cincinnati

1989 Anthony J. Celebrezze, Columbus

1990 Frank Bazler, Troy
    Leslie W. Jacobs, Cleveland

1991 Chief Justice Thomas J. Moyer, Columbus

1992 Lizabeth A. Moody, Cleveland

1993 Denis J. Murphy, Columbus

1994 John M. Adams, Columbus
    Hon. William K. Thomas, Chagrin Falls

1995 Hon. William Ammer, Circleville
    Hon. Robert G. Tague, New Lexington

1996 Albert L. Bell, Columbus

1997 Duke W. Thomas, Columbus

1998 Hon. Warren C. Young Sr., Lebanon

1999 Thomas M. Taggart, Columbus
    William X. Haase, Columbia Station

2000 Hon. Ronald Adrine, Cleveland

2001 Frederick L. Oremus, Athens

2002 Kathleen B. Burke, Cleveland

2003 Hon. Nathaniel R. Jones, Youngstown

2004 Beatrice K. Sowald, Columbus

2005 Thomas J. Bonasera, Columbus

BELOW: Kathleen Burke, right, received the medal in 2002. She is pictured here with OSBA President Mary Jane Trapp.

BELOW: OSBA President Stephen E. Chappelear presents Hon. Nathaniel R. Jones with the medal in 2003.

BELOW: Warren C. Young (right) receives the medal from OSBA President Tom Taggart in 1998.

TOP: Duke Thomas receives the 1997 award.

ABOVE: OSBA President Ray R. Michalski presents the award to Judges William Ammer (right) and Robert G. Tague (left) in 1995.

BELOW: Judge Ronald B. Adrine, left, accepts the 2000 medal from OSBA President Tom Bonasera.

William X. Haase (right) and Thomas M. Taggart (left) both received the medal in 1999. They are pictured here with OSBA President John P. Petzold.

BELOW: OSBA President Keith A. Ashmus presents Beatrice K. Sowald with the medal in 2004.

The Institute involved the Association as well as the Ohio State Bar Foundation and The Ohio State University. Its creation marked the first time that an Ohio organization had as its focus continuing legal education and legal research.

The Clients Security Fund also was formed in 1961. The idea was that money would be set aside to reimburse individuals who felt that they had lost money due to the actions of dishonest lawyers. There was much discussion before the fund was established: Would its existence be seen as an admission that some lawyers really are dishonest? Or did it show that lawyers wanted to police themselves and protect others from a few who might take advantage of others? It was the latter view that prevailed, and $10,000 was initially appropriated for the fund.

During the next 10 years, just 49 claims were received and processed; 28 were paid in part or in full, and $13,000 was recovered from the attorneys whose actions had caused the problems. The fund is still in operation today.

In 1969, the Association established the Group Legal Services Plan. This allowed individuals to pay in advance for possible future legal assistance, then be permitted to choose any attorney to help if the need arose. This plan was discontinued in the early 1990s.

To accommodate its growth and need for reliable printing services, the Association decided to control its own printing when it purchased the Law Abstract Publishing Co. in Norwalk in 1968.

Medals for mettle

In November 1964, the Association began recognizing those of its own who had made significant contributions to the group or to the law as a whole with the establishment of the Ohio Bar Medal. The first three recipients were the Hon. Roy J. Gillen, Jackson, retired from the 4th District Court of Appeals; Robert P. Goldman, Cincinnati, who was given much credit for the implementation of the Uniform Commercial Code in Ohio; and Edwin L. Mitchell, Marion, who was instrumental in the opening of The Ohio State University campus in Marion.

Significant legal changes

Affecting the lives of corporate lawyers everywhere, the Uniform Commercial Code passed the state legislature in 1961. Much credit was given to Association members for meeting, and countering, the numerous objections raised by opponents to the measure (which had failed twice before).

In May 1968, Ohio voters approved the Modern Courts Amendment—validating Association work that had begun about nine years earlier. Fundamentally, it provided that the Supreme Court of Ohio had rulemaking and supervisory powers over other courts and over those who practiced law. Rules of practice and procedure proposed by the Supreme Court automatically went into effect unless the legislature passed a resolution of disapproval.

There were several noteworthy changes made in the years just after the amendment's passage, including the adoption of the Ohio Rules of Civil Procedure on July 1, 1970. Also, the court agreed that lawyers could practice together as a professional corporation for tax purposes; that various recording devices (in addition to court stenographers) could be used to make a record of court proceedings; that lawyers from other states would be required to apply for admission before being permitted to practice before Ohio courts; and that advisory rulings could be issued in relation to grievance committee proceedings.

Fun times at meetings

Raymond Burr was not the only non-lawyer speaker for the Association during the '60s. The Ohio State University's famous coach, Wayne Woodrow "Woody" Hayes, delivered a special banquet speech at the local bar conference in Columbus in 1964, while comedian and satirist Art Buchwald was featured at the annual meeting in May 1966.

In 1965, a ladies' program at the annual meeting in Cincinnati included tours of the Taft Museum, a boat trip to Coney Island, and cocktails and lunch at the Top of the Mall.

And before "politically correct" was a well-known phrase, the Toledo Junior Bar Association sponsored an event in May 1962 at the Penthouse Bunny Club atop the Commodore Perry Hotel in Toledo. Admission was restricted to members of the Junior Bar and their guests, who received keys to the private elevator that went straight to the club.

chapter 12

Leading to a Century of Service

THE YEARS IMMEDIATELY PRECEDING THE ASSOC-
iation's 100th anniversary still resembled its first 90 years in
some fundamental ways. Lawyers still focused on key,
contemporary issues at hand. Plans were suggested for attorneys
to increase their public service. Legislation took center stage.
There were some frustrations and some special commendations to
attorneys for jobs well done.

More new operations

The Association also developed several new organizations. A
statewide lawyer referral service, complete with a toll-free
number, began operating in 1973. Callers from the 88 counties
could call the Association and be referred to a local attorney who
would offer a half-hour consultation for $10. The program was
discontinued in 1987 in a nod to similar services that were
available from local bar associations.

The Association received its first permanent representative in
the nation's capital in 1973, when it hired a Washington, D.C.,
lawyer to represent its interests there. Later, all legislative
relations would be handled from Columbus.

The Ohio Bar Liability Insurance Co. began operation in 1979,
to provide attorneys with a way to purchase malpractice insurance
at consistent, sensible rates based on Ohio experience, and with a
guarantee that the company would remain in the marketplace.
SPIRIT (now called Ohio LawPAC) began during the '70s to
provide financial assistance to legislative candidates.

Printed matters

The Ohio State Bar Foundation hired its first research
director in 1973. This reaped benefits soon with the completion of
the book, *Transition from the Old to the New Ohio Criminal
Code*, designed to help judges, prosecutors, defense counsel, law

enforcement officers and corrections staff make a smooth transition when a new criminal code replaced the old one on January 1, 1974. Soon, the foundation published other useful pieces, including *Going to Court on Small Claims, Drug Abuse Control* and many others.

Attorneys in the Yellow Pages

A hot issue in the mid-'70s—mentioned numerous times in the preceding century—was attorney advertising. In 1977, the U.S. Supreme Court issued its decision that eliminated a prohibition on lawyer advertising.

The Association quickly drafted guidelines for attorney advertising, which the Supreme Court of Ohio adopted. Ohio became the first state to permit lawyers to advertise in all media, including newspapers, radio and TV. Following the Court's decision, the Association launched its own program of institutional advertising. By 1979, more than 6 million Ohioans had seen the ads—including some published in *TV Guide*. The American Bar Association gave the Association an Award of Merit for the institutional advertising program.

As the 1970s wore on, attorneys continued to benefit from Ohio Bar Automated Research, with terminals located in the Supreme Court of Ohio, the Ohio Attorney General's Office, the Cleveland Bar Association office, Case Western Reserve Law School, and a number of law offices in Cleveland, Cincinnati and Columbus. Soon the New York State Bar Association had purchased the right to use the service, and the royalties paid made its involvement significant.

Legislation and laws

The Association continued to be concerned with laws that had an impact on it and lawyers. In the early 1970s, the Association hired former Ohio House member and Akron attorney Robert Manning as its first director of government affairs. Around the same time, several legislator-lawyers left their elected positions to become lobbyists.

In 1979, William K. Weisenberg and Robert E. Fletcher were hired as director of governmental affairs and legislative counsel, respectively. They contributed weekly reports to the *Ohio State Bar Association Report* about pending legislation, as well as providing complete and competent representation for the

The redesigned *Ohio State Bar Association Report* was launched Oct. 8, 1979.

ohio state bar

Including Ohio Official Reports Advance Sheets

association

33 West 11th Avenue • Columbus, Ohio 43201 • (614) 421-2121

Vol. LII	October 8, 1979	No. 38

A NEW STYLE OF OHIO BAR MAGAZINE

Your *Ohio BAR* magazine looks and feels different this week because it *is* different.

As noted in the October 1 issue, this is the first issue of the *Ohio BAR* to be printed at the facilities of The Ohio Printing Co., Ltd., 145 N. Grant Ave., Columbus. The printing process is now offset, a change from the letterpress method used since 1927.

The "feel" is different because the paper is different. This paper will give us a better reproduction quality for type and photos. There will be little or no "see-through" and no embossing which sometimes permitted the reader to view both sides of the page at the same time.

We are also able to add color. This issue it is limited to the cover. As we become more familiar with the capabilities of the press—and the needs arise—color will be used on the inside pages.

As always, our primary purpose will be to have the *Ohio BAR* on your desk every week with all the features you need for your practice.

William C. Moore

Editor

Ohio Bar—(USPS—404-200)—Vol. 52—No. 38—10/8/79—
Wm. C. Moore, Editor

Send change of address to Ohio State Bar Association, 33 West 11th Avenue, Columbus, Ohio 43201. Printed weekly fifty times a year at 145 N. Grant Ave., Columbus, Ohio 43215. Entered as second-class matter, October 5, 1979, at Post Office Columbus, Ohio.

The Ohio BAR Magazine is a service provided to members of the Ohio State Bar Association through their dues and is not available to non-member attorneys. Governmental agencies and educational and legal research organizations may subscribe at $40/year. Law school student subscriptions $10/year. Single copies to members and qualified subscribers $1.

This presentation of editorial opinions and statements by authors and advertising of products or services herein does not necessarily constitute their endorsement by the Ohio State Bar Assn. Editor reserves the right to reject any advertising submitted for publication.

1689

CENTENNIAL BANQUET
OHIO STATE BAR ASSOCIATION
May 23, 1980
Bond Court Hotel, Cleveland, Ohio

Centennial anniversary flyer.

BELOW: **The OSBA's 100th Anniversary logo.**

Association to the legislature. Today, Weisenberg is assistant executive director for public affairs and government relations.

Not all suggested legislation was successful. One of the Association's favored programs was no-fault insurance, but the proposed legislation failed in the mid-1970s. A merit selection program for judges suffered a similar fate as it had previously. A group called "Ohioans for Merit Selection" began in 1979—and it seemed that the idea, first set forth in 1913, might finally pass, but the number of signatures on a petition to put it on the ballot fell short. There would be other attempts in years to come.

Away from the legislature, the Association became more involved in the publishing business when it purchased the Ohio Printing Co. Ltd. in Columbus in 1979, using it to print the *Ohio State Bar Association Report* on improved paper quality and in more readable type. A new *Ohio State Bar Association Report* debuted on Oct. 8, 1979.

To the second century

The Association launched the celebration of its second hundred years with a new logo and the slogan "A Century of Service." At least 29 Ohio law firms reported to the Association that they had been in practice for 100 years or more. One of them, the Portsmouth firm of Bannon, Howland, McCurdy, Dever and Mearan, traced its beginnings to 1827.

A few months before the annual meeting in 1980, Denny L. Ramey was hired as assistant executive director to Director Joseph B. Miller Jr. He was to become executive director himself in 1986 when Miller retired—a position Ramey still holds today.

Miller, meanwhile, earned several Awards of Merit from the American Bar Association as well as the Ohio Bar Medal from the Association in 1980.

Case Hall, the site of the first Association meeting 100 years earlier, was long gone, but a plaque on the southeast corner of the

OHIO STATE BAR
ASSOCIATION
1880-1980
A Century of Service

U.S. Court House in Cleveland, standing on its site, was dedicated to remember the group's beginnings.

Those attending the 1980 annual meeting received souvenir medals and a copy of the first *Buckeye Barristers*, a book outlining the history of the Ohio State Bar Association.

William R. Van Aken, who created the record of the Association's first 100 years, died in 1993. Those who remember him say that his service to the profession was "long and varied," according to *Buckeye Barristers* editor Thomas R. Swisher. Besides his legal career, he was a member of the Shaker Heights City Council for one term and served two terms in the Ohio House of Representatives. In addition to writing *Buckeye Barristers* for the 100th anniversary of the Association, he served as chairman of the Association's Centennial Committee.

Van Aken's *Buckeye Barristers* featured many accomplishments of the Association, concluding with the centennial celebration. This was before the establishment of the Ohio Center for Law-Related Education, the Ohio Lawyers Assistance Program Inc., and the Association's insurance agency; the first issue of *Ohio Lawyer* magazine; the opening of the Lake Shore Drive headquarters; the introduction of Casemaker—and the celebration of the Association's 125th anniversary in 2005. If Van Aken were continuing his work today for the 125th anniversary, it's certain that he would have described these activities and many more in detail and with aplomb.

part 2

*preface
to
part 2*

I T IS SAFE TO SAY THAT FEW WHO WERE PART OF THE challenges facing the Ohio State Bar Association in the early to mid-'80s are eager to face anything similar again. There was, in effect, a pitched battle between bench and bar during those years.

Yet there was at least one positive result of the situation, concludes John A. Carnahan, 1983–1984 Association president who retired from private practice in 1999 and is now in-house counsel for XLO Group of Companies Inc., Cleveland: "Everything that happened made the legal role of the Association very clear and proved the legitimate role of lawyers in relation to the Supreme Court."

He doesn't want to overstate this benefit. He adds simply, "It was a bad time." Nevertheless, the Association survived, thrived and has gone on to enjoy more success, including the celebration of its 125th anniversary. It has continued to provide members with innovative benefits, including computer-based legal research in the form of Casemaker; vital and easy-to-access continuing legal education; a strong, steady voice in the state legislature; and regular, comprehensive publications.

The public benefits from a series of easy-to-understand pamphlets, newspaper columns, publications about the law and programs that reach out to Ohioans of all ages. The Association also assists Ohio journalists by providing services and resources in regard to laws and the legal system.

The Council of Delegates continues to be comprised of dedicated OSBA members, focusing on improving and enhancing the profession. Association committes and sections continue to provide members with opportunities to work with their peers on legislative matters and other legal system improvements. These dedicated volunteers, along with the Board of Governors, provide immeasurable support to the Association and the legal profession.

"We're proud of everything that we offer today," says Denny Ramey, executive director, "but that doesn't mean we're content.

We know our members, and the public, count on us to keep up with the latest legal trends and issues, and that's what we intend to continue to do."

chapter 13

Beginning the Second Century

John A. Howard, Elyria, representative of the 1978–1980 OSBA Board of Governors. Howard became the first African-American president in 1981.

THE ASSOCIATION BEGAN THE '80S AUSPICIOUSLY when it again won the American Bar Association's Award for Merit, its highest award, in 1981. The award was presented for the law-related education plans project for elementary schools. The materials had been developed by a team of professional educators in concert with the Ohio Center for Law-Related Education, and the Association administered the program.

Also in 1981, Association President John A. Howard, the first African-American to be elected OSBA president, was forced to seek a dues increase. There were salaries, printing costs, new committees and new Association programs that needed to be funded.

Electronic updates

A study that now seems both prescient and dated was described in an *Ohio State Bar Association Report* in late 1981. A survey of 38 law offices in New York, Philadelphia and Washington, D.C., found that all of the respondents who had more than 10 legal staffers were using some sort of word processing equipment in their offices. Advice to those considering adding such equipment noted that lawyers should expect to use one piece of equipment for every 10 staff members—and that word processing would not mean that they would use fewer secretaries.

This was the dawning of a coming computer revolution in the practice of law. In 1983, for example, members found that their fingers could walk easily to the Association with the addition of a toll-free number to headquarters.

Quietly effective

The Silent Partner program began in 1984. Over the years, it has allowed attorneys to seek confidential, free support from seasoned practitioners on issues that could be impacting their practices. Members who volunteer to be silent partners do not offer advice on particular cases or legal questions. Instead, they listen and provide sensible advice relating to general concerns involving family, friends, employees, partners, the Association, members of the court or even law practice in general.

The 20 attorneys listed as silent partners in 2004, including at least one retired judge and several former Association officers, were experts in a variety of areas and had practices throughout the state.

chapter 14

The Association on Alert

D ENNY RAMEY, CAE, CURRENT EXECUTIVE DIRECTOR of the Association, became assistant director for the group on March 7, 1980. He came to the Association with 10 years of professional work, receiving the designation of certified association executive in 1981. Originally from Portsmouth, he earned his bachelor's degree from Ohio University and his MBA from Capital University.

Joe Miller and his legacy

Ramey was promoted to executive director on July 1, 1986, when Joseph B. Miller Jr. retired after having served as executive director of the Association for 36 years.

Miller subsequently assumed a consulting role as executive director emeritus. At the time of his retirement, it was thought that he had served as executive director of a bar association longer than anyone else in the United States.

Accomplishments on Miller's watch included the establishment of numerous affiliate organizations within the Association, the completion of the Ohio Legal Center and much growth within the Association itself.

To a "wartime mentality"

Ramey's first years were not easy ones, he recalls today. "From late 1981 to 1986, the Association was basically in a holding pattern. We had to adopt a 'wartime mentality' due to issues with the Supreme Court of Ohio."

"The outcome of the conflict with the Supreme Court of Ohio was a defining moment," says John A. Carnahan, president of the Association in 1983–1984, "not only for the Ohio State Bar Association, but for the legal profession in Ohio."

Leslie W. Jacobs, a partner with Thompson Hine LLP, Cleveland, and president of the Association in 1986–1987, agrees.

Chief Justice Frank D. Celebrezze.
(Photo by Tom Wilcox, photographer. Reprinted with permission of Scripps-Howard Newspapers/Grandview Heights Public Library/Photohio.org)

"No one was making any long-term commitments. There was no discussion of a new building, a new magazine, or even a dues increase. We were in a survival mode."

Why? The Association and the Supreme Court of Ohio, primarily due to the acts of Chief Justice Frank D. Celebrezze, Cleveland, had become entrenched in a bitter battle. "The issue couldn't have been any more fundamental," Jacobs says. "It would determine whether the Association would continue or not. The expectation was that the Supreme Court had embarked upon a deliberate process to eliminate the Ohio State Bar Association as a voluntary organization by stopping all official cooperation with the Association."

Rating the judges

The Association and Chief Justice Celebrezze had their first on-paper encounter during the 1980 ratings of Supreme Court justices provided by the Association. Writing in an *Ohio State Bar Association Report* in 1986, Jacobs explained how the ratings came to be.

For a number of years prior to 1978, the Association rated candidates for the state judiciary by asking the full membership to vote on their competency. Jacobs noted that this allowed all the members to participate, but it was also criticized as a "popularity contest."

Things changed in 1980 when the 18-member Commission on Judicial Candidates was created and included one member from each of the Association's 18 districts. The commission invited the candidates to submit legal writings, references and any other material they desired. Candidates also could attend interviews. "Extensive independent inquiries of judges, lawyers, community leaders, and ordinary citizens who have first-hand knowledge of the candidates have also been undertaken. At the conclusion of this process, ratings are established by a secret ballot and are announced," according to the commission.

In 1980, Supreme Court of Ohio candidates Frank D. Celebrezze, Clifford F. Brown, David D. Dowd and Robert E. Holmes were all judged "well qualified." Lawrence Grey was deemed "qualified," and Sara J. Harper "not qualified" by the commission. Celebrezze was elected chief justice, and relations remained cordial between the Association and the Court through 1981.

According to history provided by the Association and other sources, Chief Justice Celebrezze announced in January 1982 that he would run for governor in the June 1982 primary but would continue to serve as chief justice until he had decided all his pending cases. He was also raising funds for his campaign. News accounts quickly reported that Chief Justice Celebrezze was the subject of a complaint to the Association—and that the Association was investigating. (Celebrezze soon decided not to pursue the office of governor.)

Even today, the Association stays true to its obligation to keep private allegations that the chief justice was being investigated and will not confirm or deny that such a complaint was filed. Several executives do state that the source of the newspaper story that broke the news was not a member of the Association's Ethics Committee, an Association officer or an Association staff member.

A surprising action

A month later, the Supreme Court of Ohio announced a startling policy change. The Association had published the official reports of Supreme Court cases since 1928. But in February, the Supreme Court told the Association via letter that as of June 30 it would be terminating the contract with the Association to publish its opinions as well as the opinions of other Ohio courts.

This came as a shock to the Association and, it seemed, to Anderson Publishing, the company that the court had planned to use for the publication. Anderson officials wrote to notify the Association president that its company had been contacted by the Supreme Court about the matter.

Association members quickly set meetings with Supreme Court justices, and four of the justices (though not Chief Justice Celebrezze) agreed to permit the Association to work to try to rescind the Anderson contract. But by then, Anderson decided it would proceed with the publications.

In September 1982, the Association published the regular judicial ratings from the Commission on Judicial Candidates. Ralph S. Locher and Blanche Krupansky received "well qualified" ratings, while John W. McCormack was rated "outstanding." A. William Sweeney was rated as "qualified," and William J. McCrone and James P. Celebrezze, the brother of the chief justice running to fill an unexpired term, were rated "not qualified."

Norman W. Shibley, Cleveland, representative of the 1978-1980 OSBA Board of Governors; OSBA president, 1982-1983.

Increased frostiness

A month later, the court withdrew its invitation for the Association president to speak to newly sworn members of the bar at the court's induction ceremony—a speech that was scheduled each year. A few weeks later, the *Columbus Dispatch* reported that a second complaint had been filed with the Ethics Committee, this about a particular advertisement being broadcast by the three Democratic candidates for the Court (including both Celebrezzes).

James Celebrezze was re-elected in 1982. Soon after, the individual who had filed the second complaint with the Ethics Committee admitted publicly to having done so.

That same month, the Supreme Court of Ohio informed the Association that it could no longer investigate grievances against lawyers or judges or prosecute complaints in matters relating to legal ethics (or the unauthorized practice of law). This was a power the Association had held since 1957. While the Association was denied this power, local bar associations could still receive, investigate and process such complaints.

Two months later, the Association filed a petition for reconsideration of the Court's action, but was informed by the court clerk that the matter involved the "inherent constitutional power of the court."

Registration fees

In March 1983, the Supreme Court of Ohio announced it would assess any lawyer who wished to practice in Ohio a two-year registration fee of $100, due by Sept. 1, 1983. This money was to be used for "investigation of complaints of alleged misconduct by lawyers and judges" and inquiries regarding the unauthorized practice of law. In December, the court canceled its subscriptions to Association publications and removed the *Ohio State Bar Association Report* from the shelves.

Thirteen months later, a court-appointed committee to study how bar associations evaluated judicial candidates came to a startling conclusion. According to then-Association President Frank E. Bazler, this committee recommended to the court that any lawyer who participated in any judicial poll or evaluation that did not meet all the standards established by the court would be guilty of an ethics violation—and potentially subject to discipline by the Supreme Court of Ohio.

The Association appointed its own expert panel of legal experts to review the Supreme Court's proposed guidelines for

Frank E. Bazler, Troy, representative of the 1979-1982 OSBA Board of Governors; OSBA president, 1984-1985.

judicial evaluations. The panel found that most of the guidelines had "serious First Amendment issues of freedom of expression and association."

In mid-1984, the Court announced that a portion of attorney registration fees, ostensibly used to investigate complaints against attorneys, would be used to pay for copies of Anderson's Ohio Official Reports.

The Association expressed concern about this policy in a letter sent to each Supreme Court justice, dated July 25, 1984, and signed by Bazler. It questioned the use of the registration fund for publications and pointed out, "We see no justification for a requirement that attorneys who choose not to subscribe to the Anderson weekly report must, in effect, subsidize those who do."

Bazler later commented that the letters could be compared to "dropping a pebble in a pond." He went on to say, "From that pebble, ripples went out that proved to be significantly helpful to the future of our Association."

Meanwhile, the Commission on Judicial Candidates continued to offer its judicial ratings. In 1984, Andy Douglas and Craig Wright received favorable ratings, while John E. Corrigan and James P. Celebrezze did not. Wright went on to defeat James P. Celebrezze.

Getting skunked

Some others involved in the upheaval also have insignia of the times—small lapel pins in the shape of a skunk or "polecat."

In 1984, the chief administrator of the Supreme Court of Ohio, Louis C. Damiani, said that the Association was running a "smear campaign" and called the bar complaints against the Court a "pack of lies."

He characterized the officers of the Association as "skunks" and said the leaders of the Association were "out to get the Chief Justice." He added, "They are trying to make people think he is an evil, vindictive man, a Mafia figure with some sort of vendetta against the bar."

Joe Miller, former Association executive director, capitalized on the characterization. In fact, he asked Milt Priggee, political cartoonist for the *Dayton Journal-Herald*, to create a cartoon commemorating the name. The result showed a skunk, complete with suit and briefcase in hand, entering the Association door. Above it were the words, "The Royal and Ancient Order of the Polecat." (See the cartoon on the next page.)

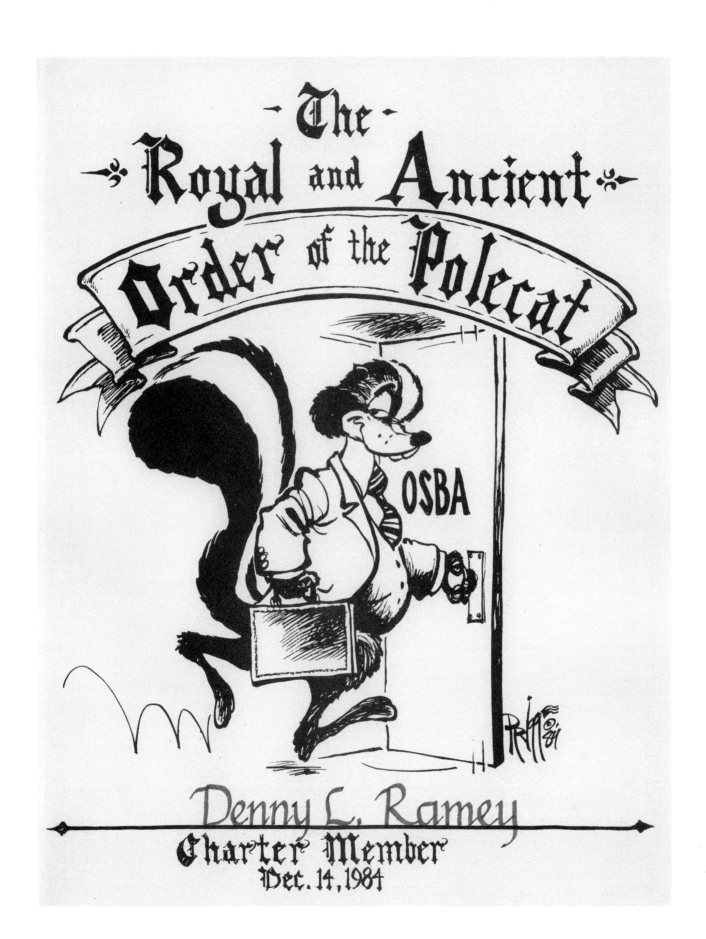

Duke W. Thomas, Columbus, representative of the 1981–1984 OSBA Board of Governors; OSBA president, 1985–1986.

Some members still wear the small lapel pins generally at annual meetings and also gather for dinner to remember the difficult times and take pride in the Association's position today.

Activities in 1985

In January 1985, the Court announced that it would cease publishing the *Ohio Official Reports* advance sheets on or after March 1, 1985. The next month, Bazler reported through the *Ohio State Bar Association Report* that there had been a meeting between the chief justice and the Association, and that the relation between the two could now be described as "upbeat." Regular meetings were to be scheduled twice a year between bench and bar, and Association-sponsored induction ceremonies for new lawyers would be reinstated.

In May 1985, the Supreme Court of Ohio established the Clients' Security Fund of Ohio, ordering the clerk of the Supreme Court to transfer $750,000 from the attorney registration fund to the Clients' Security Fund. (The Association had established a similar fund in 1961 but discontinued it in the early 1980s due to its expense.) The fund's purpose, as it had been when operated by the Association, was to help clients of unscrupulous practitioners recover at least a portion of money or property that had been taken by the attorney.

Later in 1985, discussion of a merit selection plan for judges resurfaced. The Association recommended a judicial selection system that, according to an *Ohio State Bar Association Report* article, would incorporate the "most desirable attributes" of the elective and appointive process. The article noted that more than 35 states were using some version of such a plan already. The plan was put on a timetable for a 1987 general election.

The Hon. Thomas J. Moyer stepped up to run for chief justice of the Supreme Court of Ohio.

A new candidate for chief justice

Regardless of whether the judicial selection system changed in Ohio, the Association planned to continue working with its members for a long-term solution to the Supreme Court acrimony. The Hon. Thomas J. Moyer, who served on the 10th District Court of Appeals as well as on the Association's Executive Committee, resigned from the Executive Committee in early 1986 to run for chief justice of the Supreme Court of Ohio. He resigned early, he said, so that he could establish his independence from the Association.

Significant Cases

In 1987, Benson Wolman, who was the former executive director of the American Civil Liberties Union in Ohio and completing law school, reviewed for the *Ohio Lawyer* significant Ohio cases that had been heard by the U.S. Supreme Court. This was on the occasion of the U.S. Constitution's 200th anniversary.

Key cases Wolman discussed in his article included the following.

UNITED STATES V. BURR (1807)

This was not a true Supreme Court case, but was heard by Chief Justice John Marshall, sitting as a trial court judge in Virginia, during the treason trial of Aaron Burr. Burr was moving throughout Ohio and other states to attempt to join his co-conspirators, but did not make it to Blennerhassett Island in time to meet them. Therefore, his case was dismissed. "To advise" treason "is not treason in itself," Marshall said.

EX PARTE VALLANDINGHAM (1864)

A former congressman, Clement Vallandingham, made a negative speech about President Abraham Lincoln. A military tribunal in Cincinnati found him guilty of pro-South expression. His writ for habeas corpus to the Circuit Court was denied, and the Supreme Court affirmed, holding that federal courts had no authority over a military tribunal.

BRANDENBURG V. OHIO (1969)

Clarence Brandenburg spoke at a Ku Klux Klan rally in southwestern Ohio and was convicted of violating Ohio's criminal syndicalism law. The Supreme Court reversed, holding that the state could not punish mere abstract advocacy of unlawful actions.

GILLIGAN V. MORGAN (1973) and SCHEUER V. RHODES (1974)

Both arose from the 1970 student deaths at Kent State University at the hands of the Ohio National Guard. The first held that federal courts could not set up regulations and training for future Guardsmen. The second found that the 11th Amendment did not bar suits against state officials as individuals for damages that arose while they were acting in their official capacities.

WILLIAMS V. RHODES (1968), BROWN V. SOCIALIST WORKERS '74 CAMPAIGN COMMITTEE (1982) and IN RE STOLAR (1971)

Permitted citizens to participate in less popular political organizations, including Alabama Gov. George Wallace's run for president and the Socialist party. Stolar allowed an applicant to law practice to refuse to answer broad questions about his political beliefs and membership in political organizations.

OHRALIK V. OHIO STATE BAR (1978)

Found that the state did have a legitimate interest in protecting lay people from "fraud, undue influence, intimidation, overreaching and other forms of vexatious conduct."

ZAUDERER V. OFFICE OF DISCIPLINARY COUNSEL (1985)

Struck down sanctions against a Columbus lawyer who had used an illustrated ad to solicit clients who might have been injured by the use of an interuterine device.

LEHMAN V. SHAKER HEIGHTS (1974)

Denied State Rep. Harry Lehman the right to advertise on Shaker Heights rapid transit, called a "captive audience" by one justice.

ZACCHINI V. SCRIPPS-HOWARD BROADCASTING (1977)

Human cannonball Hugo Zacchini's entire 15-second act was filmed during a fair and broadcast on TV. Zacchini's claim was compared to those found in copyright and patent law, but the Court said it was difficult to measure damages because the filmed offering might convince individuals to see the show live.

MUTUAL FILM CORP. V. INDUSTRIAL COMMISSION OF OHIO (1915)

Upheld Ohio's movie censorship law because movies were entertainment and thus not protected speech.

JACOBELLIS V. OHIO (1964)

The case involving allegedly obscene materials where Justice Stewart (who was from Ohio) commented that he could not define hard-core pornography, "but I know it when I see it...."

DAYTON BOARD OF EDUCATION V. BRINKMAN (1977 and 1979)

First, there was no finding of discrimination in the school system; two years later, the Supreme Court found that there was pervasive discrimination.

COLUMBUS BOARD OF EDUCATION V. PENICK (1979)

Found discrimination in the school system, holding "proof of purposeful and effective maintenance of a body of separate black schools in a susbstantial part of the system itself is prima facie proof of a dual school system."

LOCAL 93, INTERNATIONAL ASSOCIATION OF FIREFIGHTERS V. CLEVELAND (1986)

Upheld a plan of affirmative action, in this case where an employer or union had a "persistent" record of discrimination.

AKRON V. AKRON CENTER FOR REPRODUCTIVE HEALTH (1983)

Struck down many sections of a municipal ordinance that restricted women's rights to abortion.

TERRY V. OHIO (1968)

Found that police officers could stop and frisk individuals if they "reasonably suspected" they had committed an offense, even without probable cause.

PALMER V. CITY OF EUCLID (1972)

Overturned a conviction under a "suspicious person" law where the mere fact of being out at night "without any visible or lawful business and who does not give a satisfactory account of himself" could lead to arrest.

SHEPPARD V. MAXWELL (1966)

Established that Dr. Sam Sheppard had a right to a fair trial shielded from community bias, noting that the doctor had been tried in a "carnival" atmosphere and the judge had not taken appropriate steps to ensure fairness.

LEIS V. FLYNT (1979)

Found that *Hustler* magazine publisher Larry Flynt had no right to be represented by an out-of-state lawyer, and that being denied the right to appear did not damage the attorney's reputation.

Edward G. Marks, Cincinnati, chair of the 1986 Commission on Judicial Candidates and representative of the 1978-1981 and 1990-1993 OSBA Board of Governors.

Later that year, Moyer, Donald R. Ford and Robert E. Holmes were "highly recommended," while Herbert R. Brown and Joyce George were "recommended," and Frank D. Celebrezze and Francis E. Sweeney were "not recommended" by the Commission on Judicial Candidates.

Celebrezze's campaign manager had informed the Association that the chief justice "would not cooperate" with the Commission on Judicial Candidates. The Association was not impressed. "Our responsibility to assist the public does not go away," said Cincinnati attorney Edward G. Marks, chairman of the 1986 rating commission, "because a particular candidate doesn't want to be evaluated."

The ensuing election had fundamental significance for the Association. "It was expected that if the chief justice were re-elected," Jacobs says today, "his next move would be to organize an integrated (mandatory) bar, such as those in Michigan or the District of Columbia, where membership is a requirement for registration as an active practitioner. That bar would have operated under rules promulgated by the Supreme Court of Ohio—and those rules would have restricted, or prohibited, many 'arm's length' activities, such as evaluation of judicial candidates."

The impact of such a change would have gone even further. "It was the unanimous view of what was then the Executive Committee and the officers and staff that the election was either going to perpetuate the Association or be its demise," Jacobs continues. "Some [members] thought they were in personal jeopardy as well."

Before the election, key Association personnel planned a three-day retreat at an Adirondacks lodge to be held immediately following the election. "We knew we would either plan to expand or plan to liquidate," Jacobs says.

A winner, a loser

The difficult times ended when Moyer defeated Frank D. Celebrezze in the November 1986 race for chief justice. Celebrezze attempted a return to politics and the bench when he unsuccessfully vied for a seat on the Ohio Court of Appeals for the 8th District in 1994. In late 2004, he was residing in Cleveland. Moyer remains chief justice today.

When Moyer was sworn in as the eighth chief justice in January 1987, his speech at the ceremony touched on history and the future. "This ceremony is not a celebration of a candidate's personal victory," he said. "It is the beginning of the restoration of

Leslie W. Jacobs, Cleveland, representative of the 1983-1985 OSBA Board of Governors; OSBA president, 1986-1987.

an institution…. You need not fear discipline for criticizing the wrong judge or failing to politically support the right judge." Association President Jacobs presided at the ceremony.

A few months later, Jacobs was decidedly upbeat in his annual remarks to the Association: "The state of the bar today is excellent, far better than anytime in the last five years. The Bar Association is stronger, more confident, and more influential today than at any time in my professional career, and both the lawyers of Ohio and the public are better because of it."

Jacobs's comments today about those difficult years: "It was an inspiring time to be around the Association. People were acting and understanding that what they were doing put them at a high risk."

In December 1988, the Supreme Court of Ohio's Board of Commissioners on Grievances and Discipline appointed the Association to operate a certified grievance committee. Former Association General Counsel Al Bell rejoined the executive staff after having served as a judge on the Franklin County Common Pleas Court and was tapped to coordinate all the disciplinary activities under the direction of the Legal Ethics and Professional Conduct Committee.

On Jan. 23, 1989, the Association finally regained its authority to investigate and prosecute complaints of alleged ethical misconduct by members of the legal profession.

A year later, both Frank E. Bazler and Leslie W. Jacobs, former presidents during the Supreme Court crisis, received the Ohio Bar Medal, the highest honor given by the Association to members of the bar.

Cartoon depicting the fight between Court leadership and OSBA in *Dayton Journal-Herald.*

chapter 15

Better Relations and a New Plan

At the retreat in the Adirondacks days after the Moyer victory, Association executives developed a quick "to do" list, according to President Leslie Jacobs: Restore cordial cooperation between the bar and the Court and take advantage of the "victory phenomenon." He explains, "[Following the victory], lawyers all over the state were telling us, 'I was right behind you.'"

Later that fall, several members of the Association took time to relax on a group tour to Acapulco, Mexico. "In one afternoon on the beach in Acapulco, several of us put together a long-range plan for the Association, with a timetable," Jacobs says. "Some activities were immediate, some long-term. Virtually everything that happened in the next five years was on that plan."

Activities listed in the plan included a renewed focus on merit selection, the establishment of a new Association magazine and an increase of services to members and the public, as would be seen in the upcoming years. Long-term plans included a focus on a new home for the Association.

The plan with merit

Though merit selection of judges had been discussed and supported by the Association several times over the years, the proposal offered to the voters in 1987 was the most comprehensive that had ever been developed.

The proposed plan would include both lawyer and non-lawyer members of district nominating committees. Each district nominating committee would choose one lawyer and one non-lawyer from among its committee membership to serve on a 24-member Supreme Court of Ohio Nominating Commission. The commission would then select three names to be submitted to the governor, and the governor would choose one to become a justice. The justice would then have to receive a 55 percent affirmative vote in the next election to remain on the bench

107

Joseph F. Cook, Akron, OSBA president, 1987-1988.

(sometimes called a retention election). A local option feature would allow voters in any particular county to extend the process to trial courts.

Although the Association realized that the voters had rejected similar plans several times before, proponents noted that times had changed, and the whole concept of merit selection had not really been tested in Ohio. By this time, merit selection had been adopted for at least some courts in a majority of states—including neighboring Indiana.

The Bar Association was not alone in support of the process. Those signing on to support merit selection this time included the League of Women Voters of Ohio, the Ohio Congress of Parents and Teachers, the Ohio Council of Churches, Common Cause/Ohio, the Women's City Club of Cincinnati, the Ohio Association of Civil Trial Attorneys, and even the Ohio Farm Bureau.

The *Ohio State Bar Association Report* even included a pullout card for interested members to complete and return, indicating that they would help with the merit selection petition drive. The goal was to receive 500,000 signatures to get it on the 1987 ballot.

Joseph F. Cook, Akron, 1987–1988 Association president, made merit selection the key issue of his term. "Without any question, merit selection and voter retention of judges in Ohio is the prime topic," he advised *Ohio Lawyer* in 1987. Unfortunately, once again, the plan would fail.

"It was a noble effort," William K. Weisenberg, the Association's assistant executive director for public affairs, recalls today. "Both political parties and labor opposed it. It went to the ballot, and lost by two to one, 67 percent opposed. We knew what the results would be before Election Day."

Talk about a merit selection program continues to resurface every few years, but it still seems unlikely to be approved by voters anytime soon. Even some former supporters have given up. "It came up in a judicial forum in 2003," Ramey says, "and there wasn't even enough enthusiasm to form a committee to discuss it further."

Kathleen B. Burke, former Association president who is a partner in Jones Day, Cleveland, and still active on Association committees, sees hope for some sort of merit selection program in the future. "Now we're going in a new direction," she said, "working on improving the elective system that we have. The Association is still working hard on that.... It will continue to do so as long as we have an elective system."

Ohio lawyers and
OHIO LAWYER magazine

While the Association communicated weekly with its members through the *Ohio State Bar Association Report*, the publication's prime focus was, and remains, case decisions and Association news.

Association leadership decided they wanted more. Executive Director Denny Ramey recalls that he first heard of a "feature" magazine for a state association at a regional conference for state associations in 1985. Leslie Jacobs, president, thought the Association should create a "topical, provocative and, hopefully, occasionally controversial" magazine to cover issues and trends.

The Association quickly created a plan, developed a design and formulated a budget. The Association's Executive Committee (now the Board of Governors) considered the idea in 1986 but expressed reservations. Members worried that a magazine might hurt the *Ohio State Bar Association Report* by using articles that might appear there; that a feature magazine would not sell enough ads to make it feasible; that there would not be enough lawyers who would be willing to write for it; that members would not read it; and that the Association would be embarrassed if the magazine failed. Nevertheless, most of the committee members did approve the idea, Ramey recalls, and the magazine moved forward.

Kate Hagan, who served as the first editor of *Ohio Lawyer*, recalls, "The goal of the Board of Editors and the Association leadership was to put together a first-rate news and feature magazine for Ohio lawyers ... to cover those topics and areas of law currently in the news and before the courts."

Kate Hagan, past editor of *Ohio Lawyer*, and John Carnahan, past chair of the OSBA Board of Editors and past OSBA president, show off the new publication.

The magazine was launched in January 1987. One of the first feature articles was about the Supreme Court of Ohio. Later that year, there was special coverage of the 200-year celebration of the U.S. Constitution; in 1991, similar space was devoted to the anniversary of the Bill of Rights.

Other articles offered glimpses into the future. A 1988 article asked, "Why computerize? It's a necessity of any law office." In 1991, the magazine focused on workplace surveillance and talked of the emerging technology of cellular phones.

Ohio Lawyer's "In My Opinion" column has offered views from members on such topics as public perception of lawyers, continuing legal education, judicial reform, the practice of law as a

PREMIERE ISSUE

OHIO LAWYER

A PUBLICATION FOR MEMBERS OF THE OHIO STATE BAR ASSOCIATION

JANUARY/FEBRUARY 1987   VOLUME 1, NO. 1

A LOOK AT THE NEW COURT

Ohio Lawyer Board of Editors: Seated, left to right: Diane Florian, OSBA publications graphic designer; Linda R. Warner, Pomeroy; Colleen E. Cook, Marietta; Nancy C. Schuster, Cleveland; Jamie Pickens, Columbus; and Beth Kuypers, OSBA publications coordinator. Standing, left to right: Reginald W. Jackson, Columbus; Mary Eileen Holm, Bucyrus; Judge Thomas J. Grady, Springfield; Kraig E. Noble, St. Marys; Michael P. Hurley, Painesville; Nina Sferra, OSBA director of publications; Stephen F. Tilson, Galion, chair; Andy Hartzell, OSBA publications manager; Jessica Emch, OSBA communications assistant; and Michael H. Mearan, Portsmouth. Not pictured: Gary L. Brown, Greenville; Douglas R. Cole, Columbus; Terry Henson, OSBA advertising sales assistant; and Sumner E. Walters, Lima.

OPPOSITE: The cover of the premiere issue of *Ohio Lawyer*.

profession or as a business, and the Second Amendment and concealed weapon laws.

The magazine has won several awards, including a 1998 Merit Award for Serial Publications from the Ohio Society of Association Executives and the Luminary Award for Excellence in Publications from the Communications Section of the National Association of Bar Executives. Nina Sferra is editor of *Ohio Lawyer* and director of the Publications Department today. The publication is available both in print and online at the Association's Web site, www.ohiobar.org. In fact, all publications of the Association are available on the Web site.

Constitutional convention plus 200

To celebrate the 200th anniversary of the U.S. Constitution in 1987, the Association appointed a special committee to plan a bicentennial celebration. By late 1986, Norman W. Shibley, Cleveland, former Association president who chaired the committee, reported that its first undertaking, a 20-page brief on the U.S. Constitution, had been distributed to approximately 1,700 Ohio lawyers at committee and district meetings throughout the state.

The brief included a history of the events and a list of the individuals involved in the Philadelphia Constitutional Convention in 1787, a timeline of the convention's progress, and a list of major U.S. Supreme Court decisions dealing with constitutional issues.

The Association's 1987 annual meeting in Columbus included many activities relating to the centennial celebration. There were public service messages for television and radio stations, and lawyers worked with newspapers for special coverage and opinion articles.

Ohio Lawyer carried a special 16-page insert with comprehensive information compiled by the special committee, along with an article on significant Ohio cases that had been heard before the U.S. Supreme Court during the 200 years of the Constitution's existence.

The beginning of mandatory continuing legal education

In the early '80s, the Association surveyed its membership and found that more than 70 percent were in favor of mandatory continuing legal education (CLE) in the state. Minnesota and Iowa had adopted mandatory requirements in 1976, and more than two dozen other states had already joined them. Prompted by survey results, the Association assigned a committee to research further and gathered information from the states that already required continuing education.

Based on this information, the Association wrote Rule X for the Supreme Court of Ohio and submitted it in May 1987. The plan would require lawyers to complete 30 hours of legal education every two years and would permit education credit for attendance at local bar association and district meetings. Even before implementation, the Association had predicted that the number of courses from the Ohio Legal Center Institute and other providers would increase significantly.

Representatives of the 1987–1990 OSBA Board of Governors:

Steven Cohen, Cincinnati
Mary K. Hamilton, Toledo
Keith A. Kochheiser, Marion

The Court's final version of Rule X was very similar to the one submitted by the Association, though it dropped the required number of hours every two years from 30 to 24. The purpose of the new requirement, according to the Court, was "to maintain and improve the quality of legal services in Ohio...."

Chief Justice Moyer said at the time, "With continuing new developments in the various fields of law, attorneys must constantly update themselves to effectively represent their clients in Ohio." The new rule established a 19-member Supreme Court of Ohio Commission on Continuing Legal Education.

On the same day that the Supreme Court announced the rule, the Association issued a news release noting that President Joseph F. Cook "enthusiastically" supported it. The Akron resident went on to say in the news release, "Nothing is more important to the quality of legal services received by Ohioans than that lawyers stay current with the latest developments in case law and practice techniques. A large percentage of Ohio lawyers already attend professional seminars on a voluntary basis, but we agree that the time has come for minimum standards to help ensure that all lawyers maintain the level of competence clients have a right to expect."

Statewide "Settlement Weeks"

In 1985, the president-elect of the Columbus Bar Association, James A. Readey, learned of an intriguing idea. In Orange County, Calif., attorneys and the courts worked together to attempt to

BELOW:

Robert A. McCarthy, Troy, representative of the 1985–1988 OSBA Board of Governors; OSBA president, 1989–1990.

BELOW RIGHT:

Representatives of the 1988–1991 OSBA Board of Governors:
Richard T. Cunningham, Akron
William L. Evans, Kenton

History of the
Ohio State Bar Association Jester

For the last 16 years, the Ohio State Bar Association has had one officer with an unusual title: jester. With tongue firmly in cheek, William R. Hewitt of Warren named Leslie W. Jacobs of Cleveland, former Association president, as "jester" of the Association's Executive Committee in 1988. Duties were never really established—other than to wear a silly hat, appear at assorted parties, and play the occasional practical joke on other members of the Executive Committee.

Members have taken to the role with aplomb. The first jester's hat (in maize and blue—the colors of the University of Michigan and therefore not loved by anyone loyal to The Ohio State University) disappeared from 1989 to 2002, so jesters needed to provide their own outrageous headgear, including one in black and white with three horns. Some appeared in full jester gear (including a rented jester outfit donned by former Bar Association President Stephen E. Chappelear of Columbus at a 2003 ceremony). Some have named other members or Association staff as their "lackeys."

Jesters have been from localities throughout the state, and included one woman, Doloris F. Learmonth of Cincinnati.

"It's a lighthearted touch for our Board," says Executive Director Denny L. Ramey. "Becoming a jester brings out the best and the worst of a member—and it's all in good fun."

OHIO STATE BAR ASSOCIATION JESTERS

1988	Leslie W. Jacobs, Cleveland	1994	Eugene R. Weir, Coshocton	2000	Curtis J. Ambrosy, Warren
1989	James E. Meredith, Lima	1995	Doloris F. Learmonth, Cincinnati	2001	Roger Gates, Hamilton
1990	Richard L. Powell, Steubenville	1996	Richard T. Schisler, Portsmouth	2002	Stephen E. Chappelear, Columbus
1991	James R. Jeffery, Toledo	1997	Glenn W. Collier, Springfield	2003	Lou DiFabio, Geneva
1992	George B. Quatman, Lima (served two terms)	1998	Alan W. Anderson, Amherst	2004	Jack Stith, Cincinnati
		1999	Herd L. Bennett, Eaton		

---

settle court cases before they went to trial. Within six years, the courts were able to reduce their backlog of 13,000 cases by half.

Readey thought this was a good idea for Ohio to consider. "I was a believer in settlements," he told *Ohio Lawyer* in 1986, where he outlined a new program to be called "Settlement Week." "Settlement Week was an opportunity to give peace a chance."

The week allowed for special settlement conferences to be held in Franklin County, Ohio, in 1986, but the program grew quickly. In 1988, the Association developed the country's first statewide "Settlement Week," which was designed to reduce the backlog of civil cases in Ohio courts and cut the costs of trials.

Volunteer lawyers who were to participate in Settlement Week received special training and often received continuing legal education credit. Then they donated their time as mediators for cases pending before the common pleas courts during a particular week of the year, usually during May. The goal was to resolve the issues without a trial. The service was free.

Still operating today, Settlement Week addresses civil cases, particularly personal injury, commercial litigation malpractice, product liability and workers' compensation cases. Joseph F. Cook, Association president at the time the program began, was quoted when Settlement Week was launched: "Our goal is to encourage lawyers and judges all over Ohio to learn about the Settlement Week approach, and help them apply it to their own local situations."

According to the plan, both judges and attorneys could suggest cases they thought would be good candidates for settlement. When a case was scheduled by the court for Settlement Week, the parties were required to attend the settlement conference. The conference was generally an hour long.

The Columbus Bar Association and the Ohio State Bar Association submitted a 1995 proposal to the American Bar Association (ABA) asking the ABA to "endorse, promote and plan the use of Settlement Weeks."

The ABA's Dispute Resolution Service approved the proposal; then the Supreme Court of Ohio and the ABA assisted in the support of Settlement Week with mailing campaigns. Chief Justice Moyer sent letters to all state Supreme Court chief justices around the country encouraging each state to establish its own Settlement Week, and offered to provide Settlement Week materials. In March 1996, the ABA sent letters about Settlement Week to all state bar associations and about 120 local bar associations.

Since it was established, Ohio's Settlement Week has continued to expand, through continued efforts of Ohio courts, the Ohio State Bar Association and local bar associations. Some courts have even created simple forms to assess potential cases and streamline the process for those who wish to participate. Today, there are regular Settlement Weeks in courts from New Jersey to California.

Representatives of the 1988–1991 OSBA
Board of Governors:

Robert N. Farquhar, Dayton
Jon C. Hapner, Hillsboro
John R. Heflin, Carrollton

William T. Oxley, Ashland, representative of the 1988–1991 OSBA Board of Governors.

BELOW: Hon. Richard L. Powell, East Palestine, representative of the 1988–1991 OSBA Board of Governors.

Mediation gets its start

Settlement Week was an important first step, Association executives say, to establish the general idea of mediating lawsuits. Mediation was a new concept in the 1980s, and Settlement Week's continuing success demonstrated that sitting and talking with a neutral professional could work in the legal arena.

Mediation has since become an integral part of programs encouraged by the Association, with strong written support such as materials about Settlement Week and other sorts of mediation, including divorce mediation.

An alternative to court

Mediation is one type of dispute resolution, which involves any settlement of a disagreement in a non-adversarial manner. In 1992, the Association began the Alternative Dispute Resolution Pledge Program, with a one-page pledge provided to more than 1,000 businesses. Those who signed and returned the form agreed that they would explore the possibilities of mediation, arbitration and other alternative approaches for resolving any legal dispute before they pursued traditional litigation.

Speakers and information regarding dispute resolution providers can now be found on the Association's Web site, www.ohiobar.org.

chapter 16   Casemaker, Public Education and More

T HE LEGAL DATABASE KNOWN AS LEXIS, ULTIMATELY developed by Mead Data Central in Dayton, sprang from Ohio Bar Automated Research (OBAR), operated by the Association for several years, and was the first computer database that offered the full text of judicial opinions, as well as state codes and other documents required for attorney research. In 1965, Association President James F. Preston Jr., Cleveland, wanted to find a better way for lawyers to do legal research. He challenged what was then Data Corp. of Dayton to take open and develop what became LEXIS/NEXIS.

In 1986, Ramey and the president of Mead Data Central signed a contract allowing Association members to have access to LEXIS via their own computers or through public terminals across the state. The Association could waive the monthly $125 subscription fee for its members. Instead, members simply paid for their own searches, plus minimal monthly surcharges.

This program brought Association members business, scientific and financial files, as well as information from newspapers, wire services and other sources; government documents; patents; the *Encyclopedia Britannica*; federal law; and specialized law libraries including subjects from banking to tax. Within a week after announcing the benefit, the Association had distributed more than 200 information packets in response to members' interest.

"This was a very successful program," Ramey recalls today, "and the Association received financial benefit from LEXIS. However, in a few years, the program actually became too successful, and LEXIS had received what it needed from the Association. It was no longer willing to provide the funding that was previously offered." He added, "At about the same time, Joe Shea visited us. That visit ultimately caused the creation of Casemaker, one of the most significant accomplishments of the Association."

Lawriter extends research capabilities

"Joe Shea" is Joseph W. Shea III, a Cincinnati trial lawyer and member of the Association. In July 1983, he founded a small company called Lawriter Corp., which collected print materials from Ohio courts and the General Assembly and converted them to digital format.

Three years later, he added all the printed materials of the Anderson Publishing Co.—dating back to 1890—to his database. His company began producing CD-ROMs with Ohio case law, the Ohio code and other materials. Anderson began marketing the CD-ROMs in 1989. This was the first offering of past and present case law on CD-ROM available in Ohio.

The first disc was available to Association members in 1991. Attorneys could purchase individual discs in the library to meet their needs.

The product was the number one seller in the market in the early 1990s, and it came to the attention of LEXIS/NEXIS. By the end of 1993, Anderson and Shea had agreed to a partial buy-back of various products they owned, which allowed Anderson to join forces with LEXIS/NEXIS.

There was one significant condition, however. Lawriter could not join forces with any law book publisher for a number of years. Lawriter was left with a complete library of Ohio case law and statutes and no way to distribute it.

Shea and Ramey had that fortuitous meeting in 1995. Shea was concerned. He asked Ramey if the Association was a "law book publishing company" and was pleased that Ramey said no. The result was the Casemaker CD-ROM, with a figurative law library on computer disc.

By summer 1994, the Association was providing members that "law library" for $795 per year—far below the offering price of other publishers. "The development of this relationship saved our members money, while giving them a great service. That was the primary goal," Ramey says today.

Casemaker advances

Four years later, in 1998, Shea suggested that the Association offer its members the entire library online rather than just on CD-ROM. Ramey agreed and presented the idea to the Association's Board of Governors.

Access to the online research library Casemaker is a no-cost benefit for Association members.

CASEMAKER
WEB LIBRARY

The focus moved to the Internet. In 1999, the Association and Lawriter completed the Casemaker Web Library for the Association's Web site at www.ohiobar.org.

The library was such a success that the Association encouraged Shea to expand Casemaker to a national audience. In 2000, the Association provided the funding that was necessary for Casemaker and in exchange received an equity interest. Access to Casemaker was, and remains, a no-cost benefit for Association members. Soon after Casemaker was added to the Association's Web site, traffic increased from 300,000 hits a month to 3 million-plus per month!

Because Casemaker was so successful and because they wished to expand the service to other states, the Association, with President Thomas J. Bonasera leading the charge, and Shea developed a partnership called Lawriter LLC. This partnership has offered other states the opportunity to join the Casemaker Consortium and develop their own state libraries.

Consortium-member bar associations provide their attorney members with full access to all the libraries of the other states that subscribe, as well as the federal library. Each state pays a fee to have the library expanded to add that state's cases and statutes. And each state can share all other states' libraries at no additional cost.

Early consortium members—Nebraska, North Carolina and Connecticut—went online in 2001. In just three years, the number of consortium members increased dramatically.

North Carolina State Association Executive Director Allan Head (right) signs North Carolina up to become one of the early members of the Casemaker Consortium in 2001. Head is pictured here with Denny Ramey.

Casemaker benefits

"Casemaker puts online legal research at the fingertips of lawyers as part of their Association membership," says Keith A. Ashmus, Cleveland, president of the Association in 2003–2004. "This Casemaker Consortium of Bar Associations is strong, composed of organizations dedicated to providing their members with innovative and meaningful services."

Ohio Jury Instructions and supplemental jury instructions were added to Casemaker in 2002. Previously, lawyers had spent as much as $800 per year to for-profit companies for these inclusions. The Association's Jury Instructions Committee has since created dozens of instructions to supplement those provided by judges through the Ohio Judicial Conference. "We have five joint committees" with the Ohio Judicial Conference, notes Steve Stover, legislative counsel for the Association. "It's a very exciting joint effort."

What's there and what's coming

As of November 2004, the Casemaker Consortium included nearly 375,000 attorneys who were state bar association members in 20 states: Alabama, Colorado, Connecticut, Georgia, Idaho, Indiana, Maine, Massachusetts, Mississippi, Nebraska, New Hampshire, North Carolina, Ohio, Oregon, Rhode Island, South Carolina, Texas, Utah, Vermont, and Washington. Even though the State Bar of Michigan is not a member of the consortium, Michigan case law is also available. Numerous other states are considering membership in the consortium, and the Association hopes eventually to include all 50 states.

"Our plan is to approach the state bar associations first," Ramey said of the expansion of the program. "If any are not interested in joining, we then seek out large metropolitan bars in that state. If no bar associations in the state are willing to join, we may eventually bring their case law to the library anyway because our consortium members and Association members demand it."

The goal of Casemaker, Ramey says, "is to take care of 90 percent of lawyers' research needs 90 percent of the time. In my opinion, no association—bar or otherwise—has provided members with a better benefit than Casemaker."

Public understanding of the law

The Association has helped to educate the public about the law and our legal system over the years, but a special focus on public education, including the education of journalists who regularly cover legal issues, began in the 1980s and continues today. For example, in the '80s, the Association increased the number of public education pamphlets available to consumers; established a Law & Media Conference for legal professionals, journalists and academics; and sponsored the News Media Awards "for journalistic excellence in reporting on the system of justice, and

Some of the materials created by the Public and Media Relations Department to answer basic legal questions.

The *Legal Handbook for Ohio Journalists* is designed by lawyers, working journalists and members of the faculty at journalism schools and is provided to the media.

professional achievement in informing Ohioans about the roles of the law, the courts, the police and the legal profession in a free society…."

In the early '90s, the Association commissioned Ohio University in Athens to find out what Ohioans knew and did not know about the law. The resulting 1991–1992 Ohio University Study of Public Perceptions uncovered some disturbing information. For example, even though nearly half of survey group members were college graduates, fewer than 30 percent could earn a passing grade (of 70) on a test of basic legal knowledge. Many of those surveyed misunderstood basic legal concepts, including the purpose of a bond in criminal cases, what a grand jury does and how search warrants are used.

A majority of respondents thought that existing legal aid programs met most of the poor's legal needs, and most thought that lawyers spent 20 percent to 40 percent of their time in court. Three-quarters who had used a lawyer's services said they were "very satisfied," but many said they believed lawyers typically waste time and perform unnecessary work to earn higher fees.

To help improve the public's understanding of our legal system and the role of lawyers, the Association organized a Committee on Public Understanding of the Law in 1993. The committee decided to modify existing pamphlets into LawFacts fact sheets that were laminated, included in loose-leaf binders, and distributed to public libraries statewide.

In 1995, the Association provided the media with a *Legal Handbook for Ohio Journalists*, designed by lawyers, working journalists and members of the faculty at journalism schools. It included the basis of civil and criminal procedure and a glossary of legal terms. An updated version was published in April 1998 and again in 2002. The Association provides this book to those who attend the annual Law & Media Conference, and it is also available through the Association's Web site.

"Law You Can Use," begun in 1995, digests important law topics into an easy-to-understand style in a weekly column offered to newspapers throughout the state. Since its inception, this project has grown and now serves more than 100 print and broadcast subscribers throughout the state. Previously published articles are posted to the Association's Web site and are updated regularly. A cable TV show, also called "Law You Can Use," provided similar basic information to a broadcast audience in the late '90s.

In addition, the pamphlet program has steadily grown and currently includes 28 titles that are designed for audiences from school-age children to lawyers' clients and explore fundamental topics. Pamphlets are also provided annually to charitable non-profit organizations through a special program launched in 2000. More than 200 charities currently make use of this program.

The Law & You is a resource that provides nuts-and-bolts information in one concise format.

The Law & You

A Handbook of General and Everyday Law Affecting Ohio Citizens

12th Edition

Ohio State Bar Association

OSBA

Ohio State Bar Foundation

TOP: Law Day luncheon (to honor "There Ought to Be a Law" essay contest regional finalists) including students, parents, teachers, legislators and other guests.

ABOVE: Senior Division first-place winner Amanda Williams of N. Lima, Ohio, receives award from Chief Justice Thomas J. Moyer.

The Law & You, a resource funded by the Ohio State Bar Foundation, first appeared in 1967 and provides nuts-and-bolts information in one concise format. For many years, the Foundation's staff wrote the publication. However, in 1998, the Foundation turned writing duties over to the Association staff.

Over the years, this general consumer handbook has been reworked and expanded and now includes an extensive glossary, an index, chapter summaries and Web links. The full text of this book is available through the Association's Web site.

Association's Web site expands
outreach to public

The Association's Web site, www.ohiobar.org, launched June 1, 1997, has greatly improved the organization's ability to reach the public.

Dennis Whalen, director of Public and Media Relations for the Association from 1983 to 1998, recalls when the Web site began. "We talked a lot about the public information content," he says today. "We worked with consult-ants until we got a Webmaster, and wanted a design that would be user-friendly."

Whalen, who is now public information officer for the Supreme Court of Ohio, notes, "Our goal was to improve our public image by demystifying what lawyers do. We wanted to improve that understanding."

The Association realized that its members would benefit as well. "It was value-added for our members," he recalls, "and we looked at the Web as one more tool to provide lawyers with what they needed."

In 1998, the Association made use of this new technological opportunity as it reached out specifically to a business audience. After having heard from small business focus groups about their legal concerns, the Association developed two products aimed at helping business people understand laws pertaining to them. By 2000, the Association had published *Legal Basics for Small Business*, a handbook written by 45 member attorneys on a variety of business law topics. (This book was updated and expanded in 2004 and includes the work of 80 contributing attorneys.) A companion piece, a one-page business newsletter called *Fine Print*, was also launched in 2000. These are both available on the Association's Web site. The Ohio Chamber of Commerce also provides a link to these resources through its Web site.

chapter 17 Building for the Future

L ITERALLY, THE BIGGEST ACTIVITY OF THE '90S WAS the construction and completion of the Association's current headquarters on Lake Shore Drive.

End of an era

The Ohio Legal Center had been much praised when it opened, but by the late '80s, the Association was quickly outgrowing its home. Association membership had more than doubled, from just over 9,000 to nearly 20,000. There were also a number of Association affiliates, many spread throughout Columbus.

The neighborhood had changed, and parking was an issue, Ramey commented in his *Ohio Lawyer* column in 1988. Access to the freeways was tough, and "the image the structure conveys to the public and our members is not what anyone had in mind 28 years ago.... [T]he building has never been redecorated and some of the furniture is literally falling apart," he said.

In June 1988, President-Elect Joseph T. Svete, Chardon, appointed the Presidents' Task Force for Tomorrow, which included all living past presidents of the Association as well as the Ohio State Bar Foundation. The group with the futuristic name was charged with determining housing needs for the Association and its affiliates. The task force appointed a steering committee to study the possibilities of remodeling the Ohio Legal Center, moving to another existing building or constructing a new one.

A fine site

Acting on the steering committee's recommendation to construct a new building, former Association President Leslie Jacobs threw himself into the mission. He recalls now that he looked for months at sites all over the greater Columbus area, eventually focusing on an area just a few miles from downtown,

Joseph T. Svete, Chardon, representative of the 1983-1986 OSBA Board of Governors; OSBA president, 1988-1989.

THIS PAGE AND OPPOSITE:

The construction of the new building on Lake Shore Drive.

at the intersection of U.S. Route 33 and West Fifth Avenue. At the time, the site contained the debris, or tailings, left from the quarrying of the nearby Marble Cliff Quarry. "It required imagination to see how it could work out," he says.

The Task Force of Tomorrow's resolution, completed in 1989, recommended that the Association contract with the Daimler Group, a well-known central Ohio developer, for construction on the 6.2-acre site overlooking the Scioto River. There were to be two buildings, each about 50,000 square feet. One was built as the home of the Association, while the other was initially owned by Daimler and became the home of the Ohio Bar Liability Insurance Co. Total cost was estimated to be about $4.75 million.

Williamsburg by the Scioto

The new and current home of the Association, a three-story, brick, colonial-style building, was modeled after the Wren Building on the campus of the College of William and Mary in Williamsburg, Virginia. The building next door was designed to resemble it.

Former Association President Norman Shibley recalled in an *Ohio Lawyer* article in 1991 that he had been asked, "Why build another Wren Building when they already have one?" Shibley

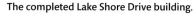

The completed Lake Shore Drive building.

The ribbon-cutting at the Lake Shore Drive building, 1991. From left, former Association Presidents H. Ritchey Hollenbaugh, Richard M. Markus, Leslie W. Jacobs, Gerald L. Draper, Association Executive Director Denny Ramey, and former Association President Robert A. McCarthy.

explained that the Wren Building, thought to be designed by English master builder Sir Christopher Wren, was built in 1695 of brick in the Flemish Bond style. It was a place for legal education in the Colonies and included as a student a young Thomas Jefferson. With this new version of the Wren Building, Shibley concluded, the future could learn from the past.

The Association's offices were to be housed on the third floor of the new building, while affiliates would occupy the second floor. The first floor would include a lounge area, boardroom, conference room, library and a multipurpose seminar room that could seat more than 150 attendees. There was parking planned for 200-plus vehicles.

Groundbreaking was in spring 1990, and officers of the Association and affiliated organizations posed for a picture with a large piece of construction equipment on April 5, 1990. The building was to be completed by March 1991.

The July/August 1989 *Ohio Lawyer* included a special insert with facts and figures about the building, as well as answers to some common questions. A 1989 dues increase, the first since 1981, would be used to retire the $3.3 million mortgage over the next 15 to 30 years. However, the Association also requested "up front" contributions from its members and supplied a pledge card, suggesting an offering of $5 to $15 per year in practice. After the

ABOVE: Former Association President Joseph T. Svete, at left, played an active role in the development of the plans for the building constructed on Lake Shore Drive as the new home of the Association. He is shown with Executive Director Denny Ramey in Ramey's office at the former home of the Association, the Ohio Legal Center.

ABOVE RIGHT: Joseph T. Svete and Joseph F. Cook of Akron, former Association presidents, were active in planning the new Lake Shore Drive building. They are shown at the former home of the Association, the Ohio Legal Center.

RIGHT: Gerald L. Draper, Association president in 1990-1991, shows a plaque to Leslie W. Jacobs, Association president in 1986-1987, commemorating the involvement of Jacobs and his wife, Laurie, in the completion of the Lake Shore Drive building. The plaque now hangs in the building's entryway.

Reception at the opening of the Lake Shore Drive building, 1991.

first week of the campaign, the Association had already received checks and pledges totaling $31,452.

Home away from home

Leslie Jacobs and his wife, Laurie, spearheaded the construction, interior design and completion of the new building. Jacobs wanted a certain look for the interior of the structure that would be similar to a grand hotel or a luxurious home. He had seen work he liked in the newly redecorated Scioto Country Club nearby and hired that design team.

No corners were cut. "We decorated with residential materials so that they would last," he says. "What it looks like today is what it looked like in 1991. Not a single piece of wallpaper has been replaced." This, he believes, is because the materials were of such high quality: wallpaper that cost $75 a roll instead of $15 a roll, for example.

"By the day we opened the building, we had all the pieces in place for a new Association," Jacobs says. "We had the affiliates moved. We had the dues increase in place. We had the finances to pay for the building." He recalls, "Once we got the ivy planted to start to climb the walls, I said, 'Good luck,' and I went back to work."

Raymond R. Michalski, Lancaster, representative of the 1989–1992 OSBA Board of Governors; OSBA president, 1994–1995.

At the June 21, 1991, dedication of the headquarters, Jacobs was shown a bronze plaque that still hangs in the foyer of the building, recognizing the work that he and his wife devoted to the building.

The $3.3 million note used in part to fund the building was retired in 1995, just four years after the building was completed. A group of past presidents, headed by then-President Ray R. Michalski, Lancaster, stood by for the May 17, 1995, mortgage-burning ceremony at the annual meeting in Toledo.

chapter 18

So Many Changes, So Little Time

WHILE THE NEW HEADQUARTERS WAS THE BIGGEST physical change for the Association in the '90s, the Association made more changes within a two-year period during the late '90s than it had made in its previous 119 years. During that time, it sold the Ohio Professional Electronic Network (OPEN), which had been started in 1992 for about $1 million, to its Kansas partners and netted a return of about $7 million. Also, the Foundation sold the Ohio Bar Title Insurance Co. to First American Financial for $19 million.

There were significant technological advances as well, including the establishment of Casemaker and the Association's Web site, www.ohiobar.org. Also, the *Ohio State Bar Association Report Online* was added to the Web site, providing another important service to members, and the Ohio CLE Institute merged with the Association. Finally, the Association staff was reorganized to assist with the growing nature of the organization and to allow the staff to be more responsive to members' needs.

"Living Will" education

In October 1991, S.B. 1, the state's "living will" law, took effect. The bill was co-drafted by the Association. Even though the law already existed in more than 40 other states, it was misunderstood and rarely used. The Association stepped in.

The Association teamed up with the Ohio State Medical Association to discuss ways they might help individuals and their families understand how to use these documents to make known their preferences regarding medical treatment if they were unable to speak for themselves. The two associations decided to co-produce a videotape and supporting materials for use across Ohio.

"This was a pretty major public education campaign," recalls Dennis Whalen, former director of media relations. He is now public information officer for the Supreme Court of Ohio. "Your

Representatives of the 1989–1992 OSBA Board of Governors:

TOP ROW (L-R):

William A. Lavelle, Athens
John P. Mahoney, Ashtabula
David P. Rupp Jr., Archbold

BOTTOM ROW (L-R):

Elbert G. Smith, Springfield
Bernard J. Wilkes III, Youngstown

Gerald L. Draper, Columbus, representative of the 1986–1989 OSBA Board of Governors; OSBA president, 1990–1991.

Right to Decide: Ohio's Living Will Law" was an 18-minute video that included interviews with individuals who had had to make those terrible decisions about life support for others.

"Doctors and lawyers went out together to speak on the importance of living wills and how to create one," said Whalen. The campaign was recognized by the Central Ohio Chapter of the Public Relations Society of America with two PRISM Awards in 1993.

The 1991 living will materials were the first in a series of educational programs on narrowly tailored issues provided to attorneys across the state at their request. Each year, the Association offered a professionally produced, 15-minute video along with a speaker's guide to any member who requested it.

Topics included wills and legal information for home buyers. "At one time, we had 40 to 50 cities participating," Whalen says.

TOP ROW (L-R):

Linden J. Beck, Carey, representative of the 1990–1993 OSBA Board of Governors.

Paul K. Christoff, Akron, representative of the 1991–1994 OSBA Board of Governors.

Ronald W. Dougherty, Canton, representative of the 1985–1988 and the 1991–1994 OSBA Board of Governors.

CENTER ROW:

Allen S. Spike, Elyria, representative of the 1990–1993 OSBA Board of Governors.

Howard H. Harcha Jr., Portsmouth, representative of the 1991–1994 OSBA Board of Governors.

Robert S. Moorehead Jr., Cambridge, representative of the 1991–1994 OSBA Board of Governors.

Hon. John D. Schmitt, Sidney, representative of the 1991–1994 OSBA Board of Governors.

Hon. Richard M. Markus, Cleveland, representative of the 1986–1989 OSBA Board of Governors; OSBA president, 1991–1992.

Representatives of the 1992–1995 OSBA
Board of Governors:

TOP ROW:

Edmund G. Peper, Napoleon
Robert W. Stewart, Athens

BOTTOM ROW:

Gerald R. Walker, Painesville
Eugene R. Weir, Coshocton

"No other bar in the country had used this strategy. Local bars were all doing the same thing at the same time in a public relations effort." The program ended in the mid-'90s as others took its place.

Capital for the Capitol

In 1993, the Association pledged $114,000 to the Capitol Square renovation fund to improve the Ohio Statehouse. This was in part because the Association had for many years in its earlier history called the Statehouse Annex home. Between 1909 and 1919, the Association had filing and meeting rooms in the Supreme Court library, on the second floor of the Annex. After a brief move across State Street to the Hartman Building, the Association returned to the Annex in 1920. In 1961, it moved to

Kathleen B. Burke, Cleveland, representative of the 1989-1992 OSBA Board of Governors; OSBA president, 1993-1994.

the Ohio Legal Center. In the mid-1990s, the Annex was renamed the Senate Building.

The first Madam President

Kathleen B. Burke, a partner with Jones Day, Cleveland, remembers when she decided to run for president of the Association—a position that no woman had ever held. She served as president for the 1993–1994 term.

"It was a really hard decision," she says today of her choice to run. "I didn't look forward to jumping into a contested election." The three-way contest pitted Burke against Stephen Cohen, former Cincinnati Bar president, and Ray R. Michalski, Lancaster attorney, who became Association president for the 1994–1995 term immediately following Burke. Burke remembers, "I took it on knowing it would be a challenge, knowing it would be work."

But she also felt it was something that needed to be done. "Women were playing a role in the bar," she recalls. "The bar was ready, and the time was right." She had established herself as a strong, viable candidate who had worked through the Association's ranks and would be an asset to its members. "Being a woman was not a negative at all," she says.

Her election brought new attention to the Association. Burke remembers, "There were some other female bar association presidents when I was president, but we were a fairly early group. I recall coverage in the *Wall Street Journal* and most of the major papers in Ohio. The media wanted to talk to me, and it was an opportunity for me to talk about things that were important to the Association." Since Burke's presidency, there have been two other female presidents, and another takes office in July 2005.

National award

The Association received the Harrison Tweed Award in 1993, the American Bar Association's highest national honor for service to the poor. The award was given for the joint sponsorship, by the state and metropolitan bars in Ohio, of a 1991 statewide legal needs assessment that found legal aid societies in the state were not meeting the needs of most low-income residents. The Association also helped fund a similar study regarding indigent criminal defense services.

As a result of these studies and encouragement from the Association, legal aid funding was increased by nearly $5 million through increased filing fees. At the same time, the Association's

TOP ROW (L-R):

Harold E. Gibson, Mansfield, representative of the 1993–1995 OSBA Board of Governors.

Representatives of the 1993–1996 OSBA Board of Governors:
James L. Hoover, Galion
Richard M. Kerger, Toledo

BOTTOM ROW (L-R):

Representatives of the 1993–1996 OSBA Board of Governors:
Doloris F. Learmonth, Cincinnati
Lawrence W. Stacey Sr., Columbiana

Young Lawyers Section and local bar associations supported additional volunteer pro bono programs for low-income families.

Women's issues

The Joint Task Force on Gender Fairness, which had begun in 1991 and was co-sponsored by the Association and the Supreme Court of Ohio, completed its work in 1993. The study included a comprehensive survey of female attorneys in law firm management, development of a legal rights and responsibilities handbook, a survey of Ohio bar associations regarding the roles of women, and the publication of a Court Conduct Guide for gender fairness in the courts.

Due to the work of the task force, the Association created the Women in the Profession Section, as well as several other committees during Burke's tenure. In 1995, the newly created section presented its first Nettie Cronise Lutes Awards, named after the first woman admitted to practice law in Ohio, to Supreme Court of Ohio Justice Alice Robie Resnick and Joanne Wharton Murphy, assistant dean of The Ohio State University School of Law.

In addition, Burke appointed an ad hoc committee on medical malpractice, chaired by Richard M. Markus, former Association president. She also involved the Association by joining with the Supreme Court of Ohio in fall 1993 to create the Ohio Commission on Racial Fairness. This task force was created to identify potential racial bias and propose methods of eliminating

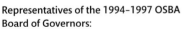

Representatives of the 1994–1997 OSBA Board of Governors:

TOP ROW (L-R):

Thomas D. Lammers, Celina
Michael P. McCormick, St. Clairsville
Richard T. Schisler, Portsmouth

BOTTOM ROW:

Rosemary G. Rubin, Canton
Jerry F. Whitmer, Akron

Nettie Cronise Lutes Award
Winners

OSBA President Ray R. Michalski presents Lucia Hamilton with the 1996 Nettie Cronise Lutes Award.

BELOW: Anthony Celebrezze presents Angela Carlin with the award in 1996.

The Nettie Cronise Lutes Award, created by the Association's Women in the Profession Section, recognizes women lawyers who have "improved the legal profession through their own high level of professionalism and who have opened doors for other women and girls." It also commemorates the first woman to practice law in Ohio.

2005	Kathleen C. Brinkman
2004	Virginia M. Trethewey
2003	Deborah Ballam Col. Linda Murnane
2002	Hon. Pat E. Morgenstern-Clarren Karen M. Harvey
2001	Hon. Luann Cooperrider Sally W. Bloomfield
2000	Barbara G. Watts
1999	Hon. Ann Aldrich
1998	Hon. Mary Cacioppo Professor Jean A. Mortland
1997	Stephanie Tubbs-Jones Hon. Blanche E. Krupansky Bea V. Larsen
1996	Angela G. Carlin Lucia Hamilton

ABOVE: Professor Jean Mortland, winner of the award in 1998, with Capital University Associate Dean Athornia Steele.

BELOW: Barbara Watts receives the award in 2000.

Judy Mary Cacioppo wins the award in 1998. She is pictured here with nominator George T. Manos.

BELOW: Luann Cooperrider and Sally Bloomfield, recipients of the 2001 award.

ABOVE: Judge Ann Aldrich, second from right, was awarded the award in 1999. She is pictured here with Joyce Edelman (right), OSBA Women in the Profession Section chair; Jennifer Cihon (left), Aldrich's law clerk and nominator; and attorney Margaret W. Wong.

ABOVE: Virginia M. Trethewey received the 2004 award.

LEFT: Col. Linda Strite Murnane (left) and Deborah A. Ballam received the 2003 Nettie Cronise Lutes Award, and Richard G. Ison received the Weir Award.

Representatives of the 1995–1999 OSBA Board of Governors:

TOP ROW (L-R):

Alan W. Anderson, Amherst
Glenn W. Collier, Springfield
Norman E. Cook, Paulding

BOTTOM ROW (L-R):

David E. Griffiths, Chagrin Falls
A. David List, Newark
Frederick L. Oremus, Athens

it from the legal profession and the judicial system. Chair of the commission was the Hon. Ronald Adrine of the Cleveland Municipal Court; Supreme Court of Ohio Chief Justice Thomas J. Moyer served as vice chair.

According to the commission's report, its primary obligation was "to point out areas where our state's legal system can improve its performance." The report provided a basis for "ongoing examination of, dialogue about and meaningful improvement in the way the issue of race is addressed in the courthouses, law offices, law schools and other legal venues" in Ohio.

The commission convened 12 hearings at 10 different sites over 10 weeks in 1994. Its 94-page report, available at www.ohiobar.org, found that there was "an enormous chasm between the perception of our state's majority and minority communities" regarding the current legal system. The commission made recommendations regarding the courts, jury issues, criminal justice and sentencing, and law schools and how they might improve racial fairness.

Can you hear me now? Should you?

In 1996, *Ohio Lawyer* broached issues relating to what was still a new technology: cellular and cordless telephones. At issue were ethical concerns about lawyers who use cellular and cordless phones to discuss client matters. Attorneys were advised to use extreme caution since there was a definite risk that others might hear a conversation, either by intercepting a call or overhearing it. By this time, some states had already required lawyers to advise their clients about their use of cellular or cordless phones when they advised them of other potential risks regarding confidentiality.

In yet another move to provide ever more benefits to its members, the Association concerned itself with law office management issues by offering in 1996 "Successful Time Management Strategies for Legal Support Staff," a video showing how a law office staff could reduce stress by increasing efficiency.

Fun and games were on the agenda when a Washington, D.C.–based satirical musical group called the Capitol Steps entertained at the annual meeting in Cincinnati in 1996. Other events in the River City also would have been appropriate on a schedule decades earlier: a reception, a banquet and a pro baseball game.

National honors

Dennis Whalen, former director of media relations, who worked with the Association from 1983 to 1998, was chairman of the Section on Communication and Public Relations for the National Association of Bar Executives from 1991 to 1993. In 1994, he received the Wally Richter Leadership Award from the national association in honor of his accomplishments.

The Association continued to be recognized for its public service efforts. In 1996, Association President James R. Jeffery, Toledo, accepted the Partnership Program Award of Merit from the American Bar Association for the Association's "Just Solutions Conference: A Public Forum on the Justice System," which had been held in Columbus in 1995.

Attorneys and non-attorneys alike joined to discuss improvements in the judicial system and to plan how to work with groups

James R. Jeffery, Toledo, representative of the 1990–1993 OSBA Board of Governors; OSBA president, 1995–1996.

TOP ROW (L-R):

John B. Robertson, Cleveland, representative of the 1992–1995 OSBA Board of Governors; OSBA president, 1996–1997.

Representatives of the 1996–1999 OSBA Board of Governors:
J. William Duning, Lebanon
Hon. Richard M. Rogers, Marion

MIDDLE ROW:

Lawrence R. Springer, Youngstown, representative of the 1996–1999 OSBA Board of Governors.

Thomas M. Taggart, Columbus, representative of the 1991–1994 OSBA Board of Governors; OSBA president, 1997–1998.

BOTTOM ROW:

Representatives of the 1997–2000 OSBA Board of Governors:
Herd L. Bennett, Eaton,
Augustus H. Evans Jr., Steubenville

TOP ROW (L-R):

Representatives of the 1997–2000 OSBA Board of Governors:
Michael C. Johnson, New Philadelphia
John M. Leahy, Lima
Terrence J. Steel, Akron

CENTER ROW:

Hon. Thomas F. Zachman, Ripley, representative of the 1997–2000 OSBA Board of Governors.

Hon. John P. Petzold, Dayton, representative of the 1994–1997 OSBA Board of Governors; OSBA president, 1998–1999.

Curtis J. Ambrosy, Warren, representative of the 1998–2001 OSBA Board of Governors.

Copies of some early brochures published by the Association.

CLIENT KEEPER

in the community to address problems. The ABA award included a cash grant of $500 to be used to support the "Just Solutions" program or to develop a new partnership effort.

How to keep a client

One of the things not taught in law school is how to secure— and keep—clients. The Association decided to address this issue by creating a set of tools to help lawyers improve their client relations. As Association Executive Director Denny Ramey pointed out in a 1997 article published in *Ohio Lawyer*, repeat clients and client referrals contribute to a significant portion of any firm's business, so maintaining good client relations makes good business sense.

ABOVE:

ClientKeeper is a package of practice aids the OSBA offers to members.

TOP ROW (L-R):

Representatives of the 1998–2001 OSBA Board of Governors:
William J. Taylor, Zanesville
Hon. Thomas A. Unverferth, Ottawa

BOTTOM ROW:

Hon. Richard M. Wallar, Logan, representative of the 1998–2001 OSBA Board of Governors.

Thomas J. Bonasera, Columbus, representative of the 1996–1998 OSBA Board of Governors; OSBA president, 1999–2000.

In 1992, members could order the Official Ohio State Bar Association Watch. The Seiko watch with a leather strap, in men's and ladies' versions, were $200 each. The face featured a three-dimensional re-creation of the Association logo, finished in 14 kt gold.

"Keeping your firm's bottom line healthy is only one of the many good reasons why the Ohio State Bar Association has created ClientKeeper," Ramey said about a package of practice aids that includes a checklist for client intake interviews, sample engagement and non-engagement letters, written fee agreements, a sample case status letter, guidelines to follow in answering client inquiries, a sample billing statement, letters advising termination of representation, a post-representation client feedback survey and many other tools.

The Association's Public and Media Relations Department and the Ohio Bar Liability Insurance Co. (OBLIC) put together the package after having reviewed similar documents from around the country. ClientKeeper remains a valuable service for members of the Association.

chapter 19

The 21st Century— 2000 to the Present

ASSOCIATION ACTIVITY IN THE 20TH CENTURY WAS A TOUGH act to follow, but the Association has continued to improve and expand in the 21st century.

A question of multidiscipline

One of the first gritty issues to face the Association in 2000 was the concept of multidisciplinary practice (MDP). The concept described a relationship where lawyers, accountants, financial planners and other professionals could practice together in a multidisciplinary office under a new scheme of rules and regulations. A big question for attorneys was how privilege and confidentiality could be maintained, as well as whether fees could be shared, and the whole idea of an attorney's independence from and loyalty to a client. The core values in the attorney/client relationship became the focus of the debate. The OSBA played a significant role in the defeat of a proposal authorizing MDP at the 2000 Annual Meeting of the ABA House of Delegates.

It remains a significant issue for today and the future. "Will law firms become larger? Will there be more 'boutique' firms?" asks William K. Weisenberg, lawyer/lobbyist and assistant executive director for public affairs and government relations. "Will lawyers need to develop strategic alliances with non-lawyers? The fundamental issue always has to be, 'How will we best serve our clients?'"

The 120th anniversary

The 2000 annual meeting, convened in Toledo May 17–19, 2000, celebrated the Association's 120th anniversary. Continuing legal education credits were available on topics including technology, business, corporations and tax, ethics and professional responsibility and litigation.

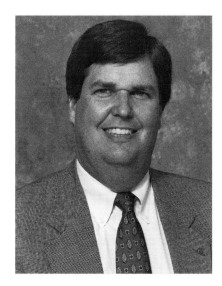

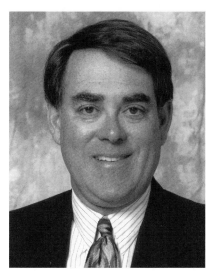

TOP ROW (L-R):

Representatives of the 1999–2002 OSBA
Board of Governors:
William J. Davis, East Liverpool
Maribeth Deavers, Delaware
Roger S. Gates, Hamilton

BOTTOM ROW:

Representatives of the 1999–2002 OSBA
Board of Governors:
John F. Hayward, Toledo
Patricia A. Walker, Medina

Reginald S. Jackson Jr., Toledo, representative of the 1996–1999 OSBA Board of
Governors; OSBA president, 2000–2001.

Both Supreme Court of Ohio Chief Justice Thomas J. Moyer and Ohio Attorney Gen. Betty Montgomery spoke at the event. Away from the annual meeting site, attendees could enjoy a reception at the historic Valentine Theater as well as organized breakfasts, lunches, cocktail parties and even a dance party.

Strength in adversity

The Association remembered the tragedies of Sept. 11, 2001, with a $25,400 donation to the Red Cross Liberty Fund in memory of those lost in the World Trade Center. Bar associations across the country agreed to provide legal assistance to those who lost family members in the 9/11 actions and later provided lawyers for legal services to military men and women being

Mary Jane Trapp, Cleveland, representative of the 1995–1998 OSBA Board of Governors; OSBA president, 2001–2002.

BELOW:

Stephen E. Chappelear, Columbus, representative of the 1998–2001 OSBA Board of Governors; OSBA president, 2002–2003.

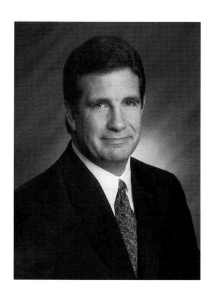

deployed to war. However, even before these events, the Association was helping those less fortunate closer to home.

The Association provided support to the Southeastern Ohio Regional Food Center, a food pantry serving a nine-county area in southeastern Ohio. Cash contributions totaling $14,100, as well as contributions of non-perishable food, went to the area, where the unemployment rate was hitting 16 percent and 75 percent of the residents received some sort of public assistance. This was a project of great interest to Association President Mary Jane Trapp, who took office in 2001.

In August 2003, the Association's New Lawyers Section, working with the Akron Bar Association, created an emergency program to assist residents of five northwestern counties after severe flooding damaged homes and businesses. The Association activated a hotline number to help flood victims obtain legal advice. Callers who needed attorneys were referred to a local lawyer referral service. Community Legal Aid Services assisted those without funds.

The state bicentennial and the bar

The Ohio Bicentennial celebration in 2003 allowed lawyers across the state to schedule special events throughout that year. The biggest took place in more than 40 counties on April 30, 2003. Judges, lawyers and students were involved in a celebration spearheaded by the Association. On that morning, the Supreme Court of Ohio convened a special session in the state's first capital, Chillicothe. At the same time, local bar representatives, judges, and high school students gathered in courtrooms around the state.

In each courtroom, the convening judge talked about Ohio's legal history based on the landmark case *Marbury v. Madison*. The participating attorney talked about important Ohio history and the role of lawyers and judges as the state evolved. The students provided presentations on local history and gave their views about how history might affect the future. This program earned a prestigious national award for excellence in public relations from the National Association of Bar Executives. Ken Brown, director of public and media relations, and his staff spearheaded this award-winning project.

Campaign spending and the judiciary

Almost since its beginning, the Association has worked for a judicial selection system that would allow judges to be free from

Representatives of the 2000–2003 OSBA
Board of Governors:

TOP ROW (L–R):

David B. Bennett, Cambridge
Douglas N. Godshall, Akron

CENTER ROW:

Kraig E. Noble, St. Marys
Walter Reynolds, Dayton

RIGHT: Keith A. Ashmus, Cleveland,
representative of the 1998–2001 OSBA
Board of Governors; OSBA president,
2003–2004.

Representatives of the 2001–2004 OSBA
Board of Governors:

TOP ROW (L-R):

Kenneth A. Bravo, Cleveland
Colleen E. Cook, Marietta

CENTER ROW:

Louis A. DiFabio, Geneva
Mark J. Howdyshell, New Lexington

BOTTOM ROW:

James F. Peifer, Springfield
Kevin H. Taylor, Van Wert

Representatives of the 2002–2005 OSBA
Board of Governors:

ABOVE (L–R):

Shirley J. Christian, Youngstown
Ron L. Rimelspach, Sylvania

RIGHT:

John S. Stith, Cincinnati
Stephen F. Tilson, Galion

BELOW:

Representatives of the 2003–2006 OSBA
Board of Governors:
Gary L. Brown, Greenville
Michael B. Hendler, Akron
Thomas P. Moushey, Alliance

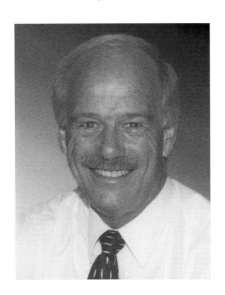

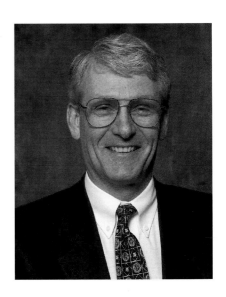

Daniel P. Ruggiero, Portsmouth, representative of the 2004–2007 OSBA Board of Governors.

Representatives of the 2003–2006 OSBA Board of Governors:
Mark A. Thomas, St. Clairsville
Sumner E. Walters, Lima

Stephen E. Chappelear, Association president for 2002–2003, passes the president's gavel to Keith A. Ashmus, president for 2003–2004.

Rebecca Widdig, Portsmouth, representative of the 2003–2004 OSBA Board of Governors.

Reginald W. Jackson, Columbus, representative of the 2003–2006 OSBA Board of Governors.

Eugene R. Weir Award

The Eugene R. Weir Award for Ethics and Professionalism recognizes the demonstration of exceptional professional responsibility among Ohio lawyers.

2005   Jonathan Hollingsworth, Dayton

2004   Michael E. Murman, Lakewood

2003   Richard G. Ison, Worthington

2002   Professor William C. Becker, Akron

2001   Michael W. Krumholtz, Dayton

2000   E. Clark Morrow, Newark

1999   Frederick L. Oremus, Athens

Frederick Oremus (second from right) received the first Weir Award in 1999. Pictured with Oremus are Mona, Weir's widow, and Robert (right) and William (left), Weir's sons.

FAR LEFT: OSBA President Tom Bonasera (right) presents E. Clark Morrow with the 2000 Weir Award.

CENTER LEFT: Michael W. Krumholtz received the award in 2001.

NEAR LEFT: Michael E. Murman received the 2004 Weir Award.

Legal Education Committee Award

The Association's Legal Education Committee Award is given to the law professor who has contributed most to Ohio law and the Ohio bar.

2002   Louis A. Jacobs and Professor Max Kravitz

2003   Michael E. Solimine

2004   Professor William C. Becker

The Association's Friend of Legal Education Award is given to the bar member who has contributed most to legal education.

2002   Wilton S. Sogg

2003   James K. Lawrence

2004   John B. Robertson

ABOVE LEFT: Michael E. Solimine received the 2003 OSBA Legal Education Committee Award.

ABOVE RIGHT: James K. Lawrence received the 2003 OSBA Friend of Legal Education Award.

RIGHT: OSBA President Keith A. Ashmus presents the Friend of Legal Education award to John B. Robertson in 2004.

Heather G. Sowald, Columbus, representative of the 2001-2004 OSBA Board of Governors; OSBA president, 2004-2005.

BELOW:

Lee E. Belardo, Avon, representative of the 2004-2005 OSBA Board of Governors.

Board of Governors
2004-2005

Heather G. Sowald, President
E. Jane Taylor, President-Elect
Keith A. Ashmus, Immediate Past President
John S. Stith, District 1
Gary L. Brown, District 2
David C. Newcomer, District 3
Ron L. Rimelspach, District 4
Stephen F. Tilson, District 5
Walter A. Wildman, District 6
Reginald W. Jackson, District 7

Daniel P. Ruggiero, District 8
David E. Railsback, District 9
Lee E. Belardo, District 10
Michael B. Hendler, District 11
Robert F. Ware, District 12
Shirley J. Christian, District 13
Thomas P. Moushey, District 14
Mark A. Thomas, District 15
Sumner E. Walters, District 16
Linda R. Warner, District 17
Michael P. Hurley, District 18

the requirements of public campaigns for their positions. Merit selection and other similar suggestions had met defeat again and again, but the new century would put Ohio's judicial elections in the national spotlight, causing the Association to take up a related issue.

In the 2000 elections, approximately $13 million in "soft" money from contributors who did not need to disclose their identity was spent for advertising for, and against, two Supreme Court of Ohio justices. To put it delicately, some ads were "ugly and disrespectful" at best. When ads impugning the integrity of the court aired, Reginald S. Jackson Jr., Association president, called a news conference and publicly condemned the offending ads on behalf of the Association. "Justice is not for sale in Ohio," he stressed at the Oct. 20, 2000, event.

In response to concerns about such advertising and prior to the next judicial campaign, the Association created the Judicial Election Campaign Advertising Monitoring Committee in 2002. Keith A. Ashmus, Cleveland, president of the Association for 2003–2004, wrote about the ads, and the subsequent activities of the Association, in March 2004. He acknowledged that in most cases, the judicial candidates had not been directly responsible for the ads that seemed misleading or impugned the integrity of the court.

Yet the Association's position was that the candidates could, and should, take personal responsibility for all ads issued by their authorized committees or themselves and disavow those that played "dirty politics."

Ashmus went on to explain that the Association had developed a proposal suggesting that sources of contributions and expenditures for electioneering communications relating to judicial elections should be disclosed in a timely manner. The proposal included a "clean campaign" pledge through which candidates would agree to refrain from tactics that would impugn the integrity of the court.

Ashmus said at the time, "We hope this recommendation will act as a catalyst to encourage legislative bodies across the nation to enact reforms requiring such disclosure." The American Bar Association was impressed, and in February 2004 it adopted the Association's proposal and urged all states to require similar campaign disclosures. Disclosure of contributions and expenditures became a significant part of an omnibus campaign finance reform bill enacted in a December 2004 special session of the Ohio General Assembly.

David Crago, current chair of the Campaign Monitoring Committee and dean of the Ohio Northern University College of Law, is concerned about the role of the Judicial Advertising Monitoring Committee in Ohio judicial elections. He says, "The goal of this committee is to serve as the public's 'watchdog,' to see that advertising stays focused on judicial qualifications and does not deteriorate into name calling and negativism."

chapter 20

How a Bill Becomes a Law— with Help from the Association

T HE ASSOCIATION HAS HAD GREAT SUCCESS OVER the years with its proposals becoming law. On average, more than 90 percent of all of the Association's proposals are signed into law. "Our success rate may well be unique for bar associations throughout the country," says Executive Director Denny Ramey, "and our role in developing statutes and rules is unique among all associations in the state."

Much credit goes to William K. Weisenberg, a native New Yorker who has been with the Association for 26 years and is now lawyer/lobbyist and assistant executive director of public affairs and government relations. Heather G. Sowald, Association president for 2004–2005, says of him, "He is the go-to person for the history of all state legislative matters within the past several decades. He is also the person who knows whom to go to anywhere across the state" to get something done.

Weisenberg works closely with Steve Stover, a Columbus native who is legislative counsel and has worked for the Association for five years, since his retirement as administrative director of the Supreme Court of Ohio.

BELOW: Denny Ramey, OSBA executive director.

BELOW RIGHT: OSBA Government Relations Department. Steve Stover, legislative counsel; William Weisenberg, OSBA assistant executive director for public affairs and government relations. Not pictured: Jennifer Moreland, administrative assistant.

THIS PAGE AND OPPOSITE:
The renovated Ohio Judicial Center, which houses the Supreme Court of Ohio and its affiliated offices, was opened in February 2004.

HOW A BILL BECOMES A LAW—WITH HELP FROM THE ASSOCIATION

ABOVE: The Ohio State Bar Association placed on permanent loan two pieces of Chihuly glass art for display in the reading room of the Ohio Judicial Center.

ABOVE RIGHT: Interior of the renovated Ohio Judicial Center.

RIGHT: The reading room at the new Ohio Judicial Center.

OPPOSITE: The Supreme Court of Ohio Courtroom.

HOW A BILL BECOMES A LAW—WITH HELP FROM THE ASSOCIATION

Bill Weisenberg was the recipient of the Ohio Legal Assistance Foundation Presidential Award in 1997.

"The Association has provided steady leadership in working with the General Assembly, and we provide the expertise," Stover says. "In the mid-1970s, 40 to 45 percent of the legislators were lawyers. Now there are 24 lawyers in the General Assembly. That's less than 18 percent." Stover explains the implications: "It means the legislators have less of an understanding of legal and technical issues and need more explanation. In addition, their staffs don't have the resources to track legislation."

He also points to the fact that due to term limits, legislators often don't have a long history in the Statehouse. "We provide an institutional memory," he says, speaking of the Association's role. Weisenberg agrees. "We aren't just advocates. We are also there in an advisory role. The Association brings significant knowledge to the process."

Looking back at his years with the Association, Weisenberg points to some key legislative initiatives. "In terms of corporate and business law, there have been revisions and updates affecting both for-profit and not-for-profit companies, changes in corporation governance and structure. Our corporate law is fundamentally sound thanks to the work of our Corporation Law Committee, one of the many OSBA committees regularly involved with high profile legislative issues."

He goes on to say, "Especially in the era of hostile takeovers [in the 1980s], the Association has worked to assist corporations as well as its employees, the communities where the businesses were located, and the interests of the shareholders. This was very significant and made an invaluable contribution to all Ohioans."

Weisenberg also believes changes in probate law have been noteworthy. "Probate lawyers and judges have worked together for the modifications of these laws so that estates can be administered competently and in a timely manner." The Association's, Estate Planning, Trust and Probate Section constantly work to improve Ohio's probate laws for Ohio citizens.

Family law is another area where the Association has worked for change. "The best interests of the child are always the paramount concern," he says.

Finally, he is proud of the Association's work in relation to tort reform. "We try to be a conscience," he says, "to preserve the integrity of the judicial system, and address issues regarding the separation of powers. And we attempt to balance competing interests in a highly emotional debate."

Stover reports that the Association proposed 14 bills for the 2004 legislative session. Members of the Association's committees

RIGHT: Supreme Court of Ohio Justices.

BELOW: The last day of oral arguments at the Supreme Court of Ohio when it was housed in the Rhodes Tower.

and sections are regularly tapped to testify as experts in support of these bills.

Besides the work at the Statehouse, Weisenberg and Stover stay busy helping others understand the legislative agenda, with regular publications including the Legislative Report, Legislative Update and Legislative Inventory. They also make numerous speeches and other public appearances regarding the status of specific bills and the law in general.

In addition to the work of Weisenberg and Stover, the Board of Governors' Government Affairs Committee reviews numerous pending bills and announces its positions on them. The positions become those of the Association, and the government affairs staff makes sure that the legislators know those positions.

The relationship between the Association and the Supreme Court of Ohio is very strong today, and the Court asks the Association to comment on many issues, including rules and administrative matters under consideration by the Court.

Weisenberg's work has brought the Association and himself several state and national awards over the years. He notes, "Always, it is the members who volunteer their time to draft proposals and provide testimony that make the difference. It is always a team effort."

chapter 21

A Sum of the Parts

NEARLY ANYONE WHO IS FAMILIAR WITH THE Association is likely to know Executive Director Denny Ramey. And William K. Weisenberg and Steve Stover are probably recognized by most members of the Ohio State Legislature and many other politicians and lobbyists.

Rick Bannister, who is from Westerville and began working for the Association in June 2000, is the assistant executive director for administration. "The Association itself has been unique over the past five years since we have continued to experience growth in our membership, something most voluntary bar associations across the country have not experienced," he says with pride.

"Since 2000, we've added many new member benefits and services, while not increasing our staff by one person. We've been able to do this by staying on the cutting edge of technology and continually looking to streamline our operations," he says.

"Over the past 10 years, our technology budget alone has gone from next to nothing to something approaching a million dollars in 2004. How were we able to do this without overburdening our membership? By careful management of resources and an eye toward how we can continue to serve our members more efficiently," Bannister adds.

OSBA Executive Staff (L-R): William Weisenberg, OSBA assistant executive director of public affairs and government relations; Denny Ramey, executive director; Jeanne Blackburn, executive secretary; Rick Bannister, assistant executive director for administration.

Yet other staff directors, as well as managers, coordinators and assistants with less public visibility, fill key roles so that the Association can function as it does today. "We've got to count on the best people working to their fullest potential for our Association to be able to accomplish what it must, to serve the bar and the public," Ramey says. Key areas include the following.

Bar Services

In 1991, the Association appointed Angela M. Smith as director of bar services. In this job, Smith traveled around the state to visit the executive directors of the metropolitan bars and the leaders of the county bar associations. She also planned the Association's 18 district meetings.

Kalpana Yalamanchili has been director of bar services for the Association for six years. She works closely with all the standing Association committees and sections. Currently, there are 42 committees and 10 sections.

"One of the most challenging things in working closely with the committees," she says, "is trying to provide alternatives to meetings, meetings, and more meetings." She is able to do that. "Fortunately, technology is providing many ways for us to accommodate our members who wish to be involved."

Committees and sections furnish many basics for the Association. "Committees and sections also plan and present virtually all of the educational programs at the annual meeting," Yalamanchili says. "Additionally, several are responsible for presenting annual

OSBA Executive Staff and Directors: (Front row) Fran Willington, director of CLE; Bill Weisenberg, assistant executive director of public affairs and government relations; Denny L. Ramey, executive director; Rick Bannister, assistant executive director for administration; Nina Sferra, director of publications. (Middle row) Kalpana Yalamanchili, director of bar services; Ken Brown, director of public and media relations; Steve Stover, legislative counsel; Char Bigelow, director of insurance agency. (Back row) Eric Wells, director of business affairs; Fred Engel, director of information technology; Gene Whetzel, general counsel; Colleen Buggy, director of membership services; Brad Lagusch, director of marketing.

Ohio State Bar Association Executive Staff 2005

Denny L. Ramey, CAE.
   Executive Director

Rick Bannister
   Assistant Executive Director for
   Administration

William K. Weisenberg, Esq.
   Assistant Executive Director for
   Public Affairs and Government
   Relations

Charlene Bigelow
   Director of the Insurance Agency

Kenneth A. Brown, Esq.
   Director of Public and Media
   Relations

Colleen Buggy
   Director of Membership Services

Fred Engel
   Director of Technology

Bradley J. Lagusch
   Director of Marketing

Nina Sferra
   Director of Publications

Stephan W. Stover, Esq.
   Legislative Counsel

Frances E. Wellington
   Director of Continuing Legal
   Education

Eric L. Wells, CPA
   Director of Business Affairs

Eugene P. Whetzel, Esq.
   General Counsel

Kalpana Yalamanchili, Esq.
   Director of Bar Services

OSBA Bar Services Department: Molly Frasher, administrative assistant; Kalpana Yalamanchili, director; Melissa Quick, specialization certification manager.

BELOW: In 1993, attorneys who were experts in particular areas of the law could become certified as specialists.

multiday programs." She also adds that some sections "publish quarterly newsletters for their members and also help draft public education material."

Yalamanchili gives much credit for the success of the committees and sections to those who volunteer to serve on them. "The day-to-day contributions of the volunteer members organized through committees and sections can't be underestimated," she says. "In my opinion, this work is the most visible and useful to the general membership."

Yalamanchili also serves as the primary liaison to other bar associations in the state. Since few of them have staff, they rely on her for assistance in the basics as well as on complex issues.

Special plans for specialization

In 1993, attorneys who were experts in particular areas of the law were finally given a way to show it. Rule XIV of the Rules for the Government of the Bar of Ohio established the Supreme Court Commission on Certification of Attorneys as Specialists. The Association's Specialization Committee completed work on a plan to certify attorneys as specialists in certain areas.

Specialization is completely voluntary and requires completion of a written examination in a particular area of the law. Those who want recognition as specialists must also meet certain education, task and experience requirements. In 2004, specialty certification was available for the following practice areas: estate planning, trust and probate law; family relations law; federal tax law; labor and employment law; real property law in both residential and commercial property; and workers' compensation law.

The Association is the largest accredited agency and the only Ohio-based agency to certify specialists in Ohio. Some national programs offer limited specialization programs.

In 2004, there were 450 Association members certified as specialists.

Business affairs

"Nothing happens here," says Eric Wells, a certified public accountant who is director of Business Services, "without coming through accounting." The controller for the Association, he is from Newark and joined the group more than 15 years ago.

He terms himself the "bean counter" for the Association. "Things go well until there's a problem. Then, 'Whoa!'" Wells is also the recording secretary for the Board of Governors' meetings.

Though he downplays his role now, Wells's beginnings at the Association could be termed a trial by fire. "I had been on the staff two weeks," he recalls, "and then I was told, 'You're responsible for the building project.'" As the staff contact during the construction of the Association's headquarters, completed in 1991, he remembers, "We had our battles with the developer from time to time, [but] at the end everyone was happy."

Continuing Legal Education (CLE)

Since the establishment of mandatory continuing legal education in 1988, the continuing legal education program has focused on how best to help members of the legal profession satisfy this requirement.

OSBA Business Affairs Department: Judy Hall, accountant; Eric Wells, director; Deborah Charnier, administrative assistant; June Sellers, accountant.

It traces its roots to the Ohio Legal Center Institute from the 1950s. Today, the Association's Continuing Legal Education Institute continues to provide useful and timely continuing legal education (CLE) courses at reasonable prices.

The current continuing legal education program is not something that appeared without effort. The Association's previous home, the Ohio Legal Center, was built on land owned by The Ohio State University, and part of the transaction stipulated that the office building would be used at least partially for educational purposes. A continuing education program filled the bill.

The Institute's first board included nine members: three each appointed by the Association, the Ohio State Bar Foundation, and The Ohio State University College of Law. In 1991, the board reassigned two of Ohio State's seats to other Ohio law schools. The seats rotated through the law schools.

In February 1999, the Association assumed the CLE function. This sounds simple enough, but "it took a long time for the merger to take place," Executive Director Denny Ramey recalls today. "The CLE Institute was a non-profit agency, so we had to merge the Institute into the Ohio State Bar Foundation. Next, the Institute in its previous form went out of business."

"The Association subsequently hired all the employees of the former Institute. Its funds and its equipment also went to the Foundation. The Foundation was the administrator of the fund, and the Association had to purchase the equipment.

"There was a fair amount of acrimony expressed by our members during the process. And it seemed it took forever," Ramey recalls today. "Now, our members express again and again

OSBA CLE Department: (Front row) Darlene Allen, administrative assistant; Jan Rose, meeting and video coordinator; Fran Wellington, director; Steve Cianca, assistant director; Jim Taylor, printer. (Middle row) Dave Gore, fulfillment coordinator; Jim Hogan, printing manager; Kerschie Byerly, text editor; Diane Arnold, administrative assistant. (Back row) Don Lee, copy center manager; Debbie Keene, administrative assistant; Rick Slee, assistant director; Dan Beckley, text editor; Jeff Ross, printer.

The Association's CLE Institute broadcasts a live satellite program quarterly to several locations throughout Ohio, including rural areas.

that the availability of continuing legal education is one of the most important assets the Association offers."

"The Institute, through its direct relationship with the Association's Government Affairs Department, has a reputation for providing 'first-on-the-street' information regarding recently passed legislation from the Ohio General Assembly," says Fran Wellington, director of continuing legal education for the Institute. Speaking of the reach of the Institute, she goes on to say, "The CLE Institute has a commitment to deliver high-quality CLE not only to the metro areas but to the rural areas of the state through satellite technology. The Association CLE Institute broadcasts a live satellite program quarterly to several locations throughout Ohio, including rural areas." Publications supplement the live CLE programs and are provided at stand-alone CLE programs.

Rick Bannister, assistant executive director for administration, agrees. "The success of the continuing legal education program in the last five years has had a dramatic impact on the Association and its members. Continuing legal education revenue represents 30 percent of the Association's total annual income—which has helped us to keep membership dues to a minimum while expanding services in many areas of the organization."

He adds, "Our legal education motto is simply, 'First on the street.' I think it continues to serve us well."

An advisory board appointed by the Association reviews ongoing CLE needs and engages in research to fund legal education. In 2002, Ramey advised the membership in an *Ohio Lawyer* article, "The Ohio State Bar Association prides itself on being the premier provider of continuing legal education in Ohio."

Over the years, CLE courses offered by the Association have become increasingly accessible, relevant and varied. At each year's annual meeting, participants can earn up to 14 CLE credits in just two days. In 2000, the Association increased the number of live CLE sites and began to offer live CLE seminars in conjunction with district meetings in 16 different locations. CLE is also available by satellite and online.

"The Ohio State Bar Association Continuing Legal Education Institute is the largest provider of continuing legal education in the state," says Wellington. "It offers approximately 130 titles each year and approximately 300 live programs annually."

The 2004 catalog of CLE offerings included such diverse topics as Internet use in law practice; orthopedics for lawyers; sexual harassment; debt collection; drafting of wills and trusts; death penalty defense; view from the bench; juvenile law;

mechanics' liens and mortgage foreclosure; and recent developments in probate law.

Those who attend 24 hours of continuing legal education in one year, twice the amount required by the state, are eligible to join the Ohio State Bar Association College. Members qualify for a 15 percent discount on their insurance with the Ohio Bar Liability Insurance Co. They maintain their membership by continuing to attend 24 hours of continuing legal education each year.

Marketing

Columbus native Bradley J. Lagusch is director of marketing for the Association and has been with the group for more than nine years. The department was established in 1998, and it works with other departments to promote Association services to Ohio lawyers. It is responsible for marketing plans, determining just what promotions will be scheduled, developing strategies, and analyzing potential markets for the Association's services.

"Because of changes in technology," he says, "we are able to do a lot more for members than we were in the past. We also find that the equipment is in place for lawyers to embrace technology in the future even more than they are now."

He foresees a time when his job will be significantly different. "Twenty years from now, for example, we won't have tons of brochures for continuing legal education seminars. The materials will just pop up on the [electronic] calendars of those attending." He also sees a time when "print publications will be gone," though he adds, "that's way down the road."

Lagusch also has significant responsibilities related to Casemaker, the Association's online legal research product. He works on the technical aspects with Lawriter and provides extensive training to members in Ohio and those in Consortium states.

Membership services

The Association has its own full-service Member Service Center, with a toll-free number, to help members with anything from paying dues to registering for continuing legal education courses or purchasing Association products.

Colleen Buggy, originally from Pittsburgh, Pa., joined the Association in January 1997

OSBA Marketing Department: Mike LaMorte, art director; Brad Lagusch, director; Angela Howard, marketing assistant.

and became director of membership services in 2001. "The membership continues to grow at a rate of about 1 percent per year ... and as long as we continue to strive toward our goal of being indispensable to Ohio attorneys, I have no doubt we will only continue to grow."

She notes that since the Association began to offer free memberships to law school students in 1998, the number of law student members has risen from about 1,000 in 1997 to 5,200 in December 2004. "We encourage our student members to get involved and acclimated to the Association early on in their careers so that they will experience all that the Association has to offer and will become the next generation of supportive attorney members," Buggy says. Paralegal membership has also grown, primarily since a new benefit was added in 2003 that permits them to attend three continuing legal education seminars each year for free.

And Casemaker has been a reason for many prospective members, including government attorneys, to join the Association. Buggy reports, "We have always offered government attorneys a reduced rate for dues, but a few years ago we began offering an even greater reduction in return for 100 percent membership from the attorneys in a particular government office." She continues, "In 2003, we welcomed the 360 attorneys of the Ohio Attorney General's Office as members in this program, and the whole office has already enjoyed significant savings as a result of Casemaker."

Buggy predicts that membership will continue to grow, and "as our numbers increase, so will the range of services we provide so that we can continue to address the needs of all of our members."

OSBA Membership Services Department: (Front row) Judy Ann Schiewer, member records representative; Judy White, member services manager; Colleen Buggy, director; Jeanelle Harden, meetings manager; Anna Wildman, member records representative; (Back row) Lynda Morris, receptionist; Cindy Causey, member services representative; Jimmie Buttrick, member services representative; Sue Miller, recruitment and retention assistant; Cheryl Minnick, law school liaison/meetings assistant; Sue Frazier, member services representative. Not pictured: Julie Neal, member services representative.

Publications Staff: (Front row, l-r) Jessica Emch, communications assistant; Andy Hartzell, publications manager. (Back row, l-r) Nina Sferra, director of publications; Beth Kuypers, publications coordinator; Terry Henson, advertising assistant; and Diane Florian, publications graphic designer.

Publications

The publications department is responsible for most Bar Association publications, including the weekly *Ohio State Bar Association Report*, the bi-monthly *Ohio Lawyer* and all section newsletters. The *OSBA Report* is the weekly member benefit that recently received a 92 percent approval rating by surveyed members. In addition to Association publications, the publications department is responsible for managing all content on the Association Web site.

Ohio Lawyer is the Association's bi-monthly award-winning news and feature magazine that examines legal trends and issues through regular articles and columns. It offers columns on professional ethics, legislative issues and legal Web sites, as well as OSBA news, activities and updates from the OSBA president and executive director. The *Ohio Lawyer* Board of Editors, which is comprised of six members of the Board of Governors and six other volunteer members, reviews submitted articles and helps plan the issues, and Nina Sferra serves as the editor of the magazine.

Sferra is director of publications and has been with the Association for more than five years. According to Sferra, "Because of technology, we are able to take publications to a whole new level—the OSBA Web site." All publications are posted to the Web, and some are e-mailed to members, such as the *Ohio State Bar Association Report Online*, which the Association began offering to members in 2001.

Public relations

The Association has had a strong public and media relations program for decades. News releases cover Association activities as well as legal topics of more general interest such as pro bono activities or statewide legal initiatives.

The Association has developed and maintains excellent and open relationships with the Ohio media. In addition to providing Association news, the public and media relations arm of the Association serves as a resource for members of the working press, providing information and "human" resources—our members—for the media.

The Legal Eagle program, developed in 2001 by Ken Brown, current director of public and media relations, assists the bar in

OSBA Public and Media Relations Department: Jessica Emch, communications assistant; Ken Brown, director; Debby Cooper, public information manager.

expressing legal ideas to the public and allows television and radio stations ready access to experts on issues in the news. This program has garnered several professional awards.

The weekly programs, which have aired on a half-dozen television stations as well as several radio stations, are partnerships among the Association, the local media outlets and local lawyers. The local bar association chooses the topics, provides local lawyers to appear on air, and provides news anchors with background information to use in the interviews.

Each segment includes the link to the Association's Web site. Viewers can also find names and contact information for attorneys in their own areas. A strong secondary benefit is that local and metropolitan bar associations also benefit from this exposure.

Legal Eagle is operated at no cost to the Association or to the television or radio station. It was listed in the 2002 Associations Advance America Honor Roll and received the National Association of Bar Executives Community and Educational Outreach Award in 2002.

In late 2004, the Association received a Luminary Award for Excellence in Public Relations from the National Association of Bar Executives in Minneapolis, Minn. The project involved judges, lawyers and students participating in the state's bicentennial activities, and the national association termed it a "textbook public relations program." Brown received the award on behalf of the Association.

During Law Week in May, students who have qualified for state competition are invited to Columbus for a luncheon with parents, teachers, legislators and others. Since the contest's inception, Chief Justice Thomas J. Moyer has addressed luncheon attendees, and on one occasion, he participated in contest judging. To help prepare students for the contest and teach them about the lawmaking process, attorneys across the state volunteer to visit classrooms.

Technology

The Association staff is justifiably proud of Casemaker, and that certainly includes Fred Engel, director of technology. From Chillicothe, he joined the Association in 1998. "We took Casemaker from CD-ROM and brought it online."

Regarding Casemaker's technological evolution, he explains, "Originally, it was just us doing it in the information technology department. Now there's a full-time staff at Lawriter, and that's all they do. We are really proud of it and the fact we really put it together." Databases in Casemaker continue to expand to include more and more states—and more and more information—on a regular basis.

Engel also points to the success of the electronic version of the *Ohio State Bar Association Report*. "We send out 17,000 to 18,000 'books' each Friday via e-mail," he says, "while the hard copy book may come Saturday or the following week. Because we don't have the space limitations of the book, we have better summaries than can fit on the back of the book. And you can click on a case and go right into Casemaker."

Of course, the most profound technology provision for the Association members was the creation of the Web site, www.ohiobar.org, on June 1, 1997. Here, clients, members of the public, judges, members of the Association and others can find comprehensive information on everything from the law and lawyers to Ohio legislative news and information about educational programs for teachers and students.

He predicts even bigger and better things for his department and for the www.ohiobar.org Web site. In 2005, the site should also include summaries of reported and "unreported" cases from the Supreme Court of Ohio as well as the appellate courts. "We're also looking into electronic forms and standardized forms for courts that can be filled out more easily." Client education materials and other documents will also be added to the Web site library.

OSBA Technology Department: John Elrod, Web designer/network engineer; Joseph Brancato, network administrator; Shane Zatezalo, Webmaster/senior programmer/ network engineer; Fred Engel, director.

OSBA General Counsel Department:
Paula Hickey, administrative assistant;
Eugene Whetzel, general counsel.

Down the road, Engel looks forward to the institution of the Ohio Court Network Program. Expected in 2006 or 2007, it will allow courts to be linked so that a judge in one county will be able to call up information about cases in other counties through one portal.

Lawyer discipline and the unauthorized practice of law: Protection and service

Rule V of the Rules of the Government of the Bar of Ohio controls the state's system of lawyer discipline. In 1995, the Association formed what was commonly called the Bell Commission after longtime Association General Counsel Albert L. Bell. He and his Commission labored for two years on a report recommending changes to Rule V. The changes took effect Sept. 1, 1999.

Eugene P. Whetzel, a native of Republic, Pa., joined the Association staff in 1993 and now serves as general counsel. During the Celebrezze era, the Association's ability to investigate grievance matters was revoked. When Chief Justice Moyer took office, the Association re-established the grievance powers of the Legal Ethics and Professional Conduct Committee.

Whetzel is counsel to the Certified Grievance Committee as well as to the Unauthorized Practice of Law Committee. The UPL committee was established to protect the public. "We must continue to enhance our role in combating the unauthorized practice of law," Whetzel said. He praises the lawyers with whom he works, both in grievance and UPL matters. "The tremendous quality of the volunteer work impresses me," he says. "They are some of the best lawyers I have ever met, and the Association could not function without them."

He expects the unauthorized practice of law to increase because of technology and the activities of unscrupulous Internet providers and various franchises. For example, he points to "trust mills" and explains how such operations work: "They call seniors and convince them to pay $2,000 for a trust that they don't need or could have received from a competent lawyer for half that price."

Much of Whetzel's work is in education of the public and of practitioners. "Even though I cannot give legal advice, I spend a good deal of time on the phone talking about ethical issues."

Ohio State Bar Association has nine employees with 15 or more years of service:

June Sellers, accountant, 17 years

Terry Henson, advertising sales assistant, 19 years

Sue Miller, administrative assistant, 19 years

Jeanne Blackburn, executive secretary, 21 years

Judy White, member services manager, 23 years

Denny Ramey, executive director, 25 years

Judy Hall, accountant, 26 years

William Weisenberg, lawyer/lobbyist, assistant executive director for public affairs, 26 years

Don Lee, copy center manager, 39 years

chapter *22*

The Affiliates

The ASSOCIATION HAS A NUMBER OF AFFILIATED organizations. Some are for-profit, some are non-profit. Each has its own board or other entity in charge. The Association has input into the makeup of the boards, but it does not control the affiliates. Each organization has been developed for a specific purpose, to help the bar or the public. Following is some information about each one.

OPEN/OHIO PROFESSIONAL
ELECTRONIC NETWORK

This affiliate was sold by the Association in 1998 but still deserves mention. Before there was an Ohio Professional Electronic Network (OPEN), Ohio lawyers could get copies of county arrest records, driver license abstracts and legislative information only if they were willing to spend enough time and money and wait days or weeks for the results. After OPEN's establishment, this data could be available in minutes.

In 1993, Association President H. Ritchey Hollenbaugh, Columbus, appointed Marjory Pizzuti to be chief executive officer of the Ohio Professional Electronic Network. It was a joint venture between the Association and Professional Electronic Networks, a Kansas-based company. The newly formed network came into existence after more than three years' work by Association staff and board in response to the members' request to provide faster, more efficient computer access to public records databases they needed for their practices.

A year later, the Association had invested $1.1 million in the operation. It gave lawyers, bankers, human resources and security managers, and other professionals online access to state and local public records information.

Two years later, the network already had 4,000 subscribers, half of them in the legal profession. It included access to two different Bureau of Motor Vehicles databases, including driver license abstracts and vehicle registrations, two secretary of state databases, county arrest records in most of Ohio as well as part of Michigan and Indiana, the Industrial Commission adjudication system and Ohio legislative information.

OPEN also added a public records order system, allowing subscribers to request copies of state and county Uniform Commercial Code filings, tax liens, judgments and pending suits. Court dispositions were added soon after.

In Franklin County, court docket information was available online through OPEN. The network was to be expanded to include domestic, civil and criminal docket files. OPEN required, not surprisingly, a personal computer and a modem. A printer was optional. Cost was generally well within an attorney's budget.

The Association's relationship with OPEN prospered. Association President Richard Markus, Denny Ramey, Assistant Executive Director Kate Hagan, and OPEN Chief Executive Officer Dick Lippert ensured that the company grew and prospered in the mid-1990s.

In 1997, the Kansas partners asked the Association to help to make OPEN a national program. This was going to cost the Association much more than its initial $1.1 million investment. The Board of Governors considered the options and decided that it could not justify such a significant financial expense for an operation that did not have a lot to do with the Association's core activities. The Board authorized Markus to negotiate a buyout with the Kansas partners.

In May 1998, OPEN offered a cash buyout of $7 million. The Association accepted, and the sale was finalized at the end of June. The single greatest amount of cash was added to the Association's coffers since its establishment in 1880. The buyout essentially doubled the Association's cash reserves.

A special committee chaired by Tom Taggart, past Association president, developed a plan for investing the proceeds from the OPEN buyout. One immediate benefit: The influx of money meant the Association would not need to raise its dues.

The Ohio Bar Title Insurance Co.

The Ohio Bar Title Insurance Co. is no longer an affiliate, either, but is equally worthy of mention. It was incorporated on July 27, 1953, as a for-profit company.

There were two classes of stock. The foundation owned all the voting shares, and other shares were sold in an effort to raise funds. These shares were widely available, and their purchase promoted.

Over the years, some of those shares were donated to the foundation, but most remained in the hands of private individuals. By 1993, it was the fourth largest underwriter of title insurance in the state and expanded its sales to northeastern Ohio. A significant strength was the fact that the company was run by lawyers for lawyers and the public.

In 1999, in an attempt to refocus on fundamental legal issues and to obtain funds, the foundation sold the Ohio Bar Title Insurance Co. to First American Title Insurance Co. for $19 million. At that time, a few more individuals or their estates donated shares of the company to the foundation, but the majority were redeemed by the title company directly from the shareholders, Linda Thompson Kohli, executive director of the foundation, says.

OHIO LEGAL SERVICE FUND INC.

The Ohio Legal Service Fund, begun in 1975, was a prepaid legal services plan that allowed those who participated to select any attorney they chose to assist with legal issues. Clients of the program included the City of Columbus, which provided the fund coverage as a benefit to its employees; the Columbus Zoo; the Grove City police officers; and both Madison and Franklin townships.

The fund lost popularity, however, as employees requested other benefits instead of prepaid legal services and some unions preferred to have employees work with specific lawyers of the unions' choosing. It is no longer in existence.

THE OHIO STATE BAR FOUNDATION

The Ohio State Bar Foundation is the philanthropic arm of the Association and is the oldest of the affiliate organizations. It was formed in 1951 to raise money to build the Ohio Legal Center building. It is a 501(c)(3) charitable organization whose members include attorneys and judges, and it is dedicated to the mission of promoting public understanding of the law and improvements in the justice system throughout Ohio.

Ohio State Bar Foundation: From left to right: Britani Bishop, intern; Jacob Smith, intern; Staci Van Leeuwen, operations manager; Stuart Cordell, immediate past president; Linda Thompson Kohli, executive director; Beth Gillespie, program and events manager; Laralyn Sasaki, associate executive director.

Since 1991, the foundation has awarded more than $2 million in grants. Recent awards include:

- $5,000 to the Akron Bar Association for Street Law and Camp Law;
- $24,518 for the state Supreme Court's Ohio Drug Court education video project;
- Up to $72,000 for the Association's new lawyer training program;
- $39,995 for University of Cincinnati key initiative Focus Research Project;
- $25,000 for Ohio Hospice and Palliative Care Organization Advance Health Care Directives Project;
- $30,000 for ProKids, to teach Court-Appointed Special Advocate volunteers to deal with domestic violence and abuse cases;
- $25,000 for Community Refugee and Immigration Services;
- $11,000 to translate the Association's LawFacts into Spanish; and
- $2,700 for Women's Re-Entry, to create educational materials to help women inmates facing child custody issues.

The foundation has been awarding scholarships and grants since the 1950s. It is a member of the Ohio Grantmakers Forum and abides by the code of ethics of the Council of Foundations. Linda Thompson Kohli is executive director of the foundation.

THE OHIO CENTER FOR LAW-RELATED EDUCATION

In 1987, the Association joined the American Civil Liberties Union and the Ohio Attorney General in sponsoring a statewide high school mock trial program. The Supreme Court of Ohio became a sponsor in June 1988.

Ohio Mock Trial initially included 28 schools. The first year, students tackled a constitutional issue involving a basketball player who was sightless in one eye and had been denied the right to play on the school's team due to his condition.

In 1989, the Ohio Mock Trial Program officially became the Ohio Center for Law-Related Education (OCLRE) and was granted 501(c)(3) tax status. In addition to the Mock Trial Program,

the center now includes many other programs, such as a statewide annual law and citizenship conference for teachers, numerous teacher workshops and a Youth for Justice program. Today, the Ohio Mock Trial program is the largest non-athletic extracurricular program in Ohio's schools.

The Association donates the space at headquarters that is used by the center, and Deborah DeHaan serves as executive director of OCLRE.

Teams from across Ohio

Currently there are more than 400 mock trial teams, from nearly 300 Ohio schools in 30 districts, participating in mock trial events. Forty-eight teams compete at the state level each year.

Topics continue to be significant and relevant. In the 2004–2005 school year, the case was *Biotex Labs LLC v. The Animal Rights Foundation* (ARF). The lab, which does biological testing for food, drug and cosmetic companies, has accepted a contract to test a nerve gas antidote on rabbits and guinea pigs, which would have to be destroyed after the test. The ARF publicized this information on its Web site, and thereafter Biotex suffered a break-in with destruction of files and equipment and hundreds of animals released. Question: Was the foundation responsible for the attack and destruction?

Ohio Center for Law-Related Education:
(Front row) Cindy Previte, database manager; Deborah DeHaan, executive director; Kate Strickland, program assistant. (Back row) Mike Sammons, operations director; Suzanne Besanceney, program assistant; Betsy McNabb, program assistant; Jared Reitz, program director.

BELOW: Participants in a Mock Trial program in 1990.

BELOW RIGHT: Jared Reitz, OCLRE program director, poses with attendees at the Camp and Academy.

Students swear in at Mock Trial.

Middle schoolers participate, too

The Middle School Mock Trial Program, first tested in the 2000–2001 school year in the Columbus gifted and talented program, allows middle school students around the state to adjudicate cases based on books normally read in their schools. Individual teachers choose whether to conduct the program as a competition. The finals for the 2004–2005 program were held in late April 2005 at the Statehouse.

The center also schedules annual conferences on law and citizenship for teachers. In 2004, the 14th annual conference included such topics as law and careers; street law for street kids; presidential decisions in times of peace and war; meeting middle school social studies standards using the newspaper; saluting Ohio's first ladies; and war of the worlds: media and law.

OHIO GOVERNMENT IN ACTION

A two-day workshop, "Ohio Government in Action," helps students understand Ohio's executive branch of government from the people who run it. "Project Citizen" is a program designed for students in 5th through 8th grades to promote youth participation in state and local government.

"Youth for Justice" is part of a national program primarily to promote safe and drug-free schools and communities. Students in the 5th through 8th grades research problems in their schools and communities, then suggest ways to solve them. A spring summit in Columbus allows students to present their findings and recommend solutions. The information goes to other students, legislators, community leaders, educators and others. Funding for Youth for Justice comes from the Ohio State Bar Foundation as well as the Ohio Office of Criminal Justice Services and the Chicago Constitutional Rights Foundation.

The Ohio Center for Law-Related Education has developed a program to teach elementary, middle and high school students about the history and principles of constitutional democracy. Faux congressional hearings are part of the curriculum. In high school, students can enter a competition where constitutional knowledge is tested. The most recent competition was in late January 2005 at the Statehouse.

OBLIC: Seated, left to right, Roger Pence, IT director; Angela Poe, assistant underwriter; George Krempley, president; Frederick Hunker, vice president of claims; and Linda Sautter, corporate secretary. Standing, left to right, Antionette Goff, systems programmer; Carol Ross, data entry; Carrie Anthony, secretary; Gretchen Koehler Mote, director of loss prevention; Christine Paynter, assistant bookkeeper; and Carolyn Crabtree, underwriter.

OHIO BAR LIABILITY INSURANCE CO.

In the mid-'70s, the Association sponsored a lawyers' professional liability insurance program offered by the American Bankers Insurance Co. of Florida. American Bankers and American Home Assurance Co. were the only two carriers of legal liability insurance in the market at that time.

In 1975, American Bankers proposed a rate increase and implied it might withdraw from the market if the increase was not granted. The Association permitted the increase, but at the same time the Executive Committee (now the Board of Governors) discussed establishing its own malpractice insurance company. After just a month, the plan was shelved as too expensive. A year later, American Bankers asked for another rate increase. Its request was not negotiable, and the company refused to guarantee the new rates for even one year.

This was not sitting well with Ohio attorneys, since total malpractice insurance claims in Ohio were added to claims throughout the country to determine the premium. But Ohio's number accounted for just 20 percent of the premium; 80 percent of the premium was determined based on national experience.

Jay B. Ellis, then-director of Professional Services for the Association, outlined the problem in a 1977 issue of the *Ohio State Bar Association Report*, calling soaring premiums a "crisis" in the market. Another rate increase came a year later.

Association member support for its own liability company

A survey sent to Association members in 1978 found that 88 percent of the respondents supported the idea of a professional liability company operated by the Association. More research was completed, and Columbus attorney John M. Adams, president of the Association in 1978, appointed a steering committee to consider the idea.

On August 30, 1978, the name was chosen, and its articles of incorporation were filed on Dec. 5, 1978. James R. Burchfield, then a principal in the Columbus firm of Burchfield Smith and Nelson, became the first president of the Ohio Bar Liability

Insurance Co. The Association withdrew its support of the American Bankers Insurance plan in December 1978.

Association members received the details about the insurance company at a January 1979 meeting. Run by lawyers, for lawyers, coverage was offered on a "claims made" basis. Coverage was for damages from professional services that were provided, or should have been provided, by an individual and his or her employees as a lawyer and/or as a notary public.

The newly formed company also made available coverage for services performed in a lawyer-client relationship by a lawyer, even though such services could have been performed by a non-lawyer. The company supplied coverage for personal injury actions, such as claims for false arrest, libel and slander. It also could provide coverage for prior acts as well as for acts, errors or omissions causing a claim that occurred during the term of the policy but reported after the policy was terminated.

Essential and important coverage

Coverage offered by the liability insurance company was similar to coverage written by commercial companies with competitive rates. By August 29, 1979, the company had sold enough stock that it could begin operation, selling property and casualty insurance. In October, the announcement went out to Association members that it had been licensed to sell professional liability insurance, and a month later, more than 100 policies had been written, with premiums in excess of $100,000.

Albert G. Slakis, a Cincinnatian with years of experience in the insurance industry, was hired as chief executive officer in November 1979. He was one of the few non-attorneys in key roles at the company. He retired in January 2003. Current chief officer is George D. Krempley, a native of Chicago.

The liability insurance company is one of the first companies in the country formed solely to provide professional liability insurance to lawyers. Its rates are set based on experience with similar claims in Ohio—rather than with the entire country. Over the years, a number of other organizations with a similar purpose have been formed in other states.

Association takes ownership of liability insurance company

In early years, "Class A" shares had been sold to members of the bar, and "Class B" shares were sold to the Association. In

1999, the Class A shares were redeemed by the insurance company, which left the Association as the sole owner of the company. The company is housed next door to the Association in a building that it owns and is very similar to its home.

OHIO STATE BAR ASSOCIATION INSURANCE AGENCY

Professional liability insurance is just one type of insurance available to members of the Association through its affiliates. The Ohio State Bar Association Insurance Agency was established in 1998 as a service to members and is also an Association affiliate.

It offers:

- Health insurance;
- Dental insurance;
- Disability income insurance;
- Life insurance;
- Business overhead expense insurance;
- Long-term care insurance; and
- Bonds.

Charlene Bigelow joined the agency in February 2002 and became general agent of the Association's insurance agency in August 2002. There are three licensed staff members in the agency to serve Association members.

Speaking about the agency's status, Bigelow says, "The Bar Association Insurance Agency filed with the Ohio Department of Insurance to become a HealthCare Alliance." She explains, "Becoming a HealthCare Alliance allows for tax breaks on health insurance premiums as well as lower and more manageable health insurance premium renewals. There are only a few HealthCare Alliances in the state of Ohio, and we're happy that the Bar Association is one of them." The insurance agency expanded its health carriers in 2002 and now works with all major carriers in Ohio.

OSBA Insurance Agency: Char Bigelow, director; Tammy Thornton, insurance sales. Not pictured: Penny Peitsmeyer, insurance sales.

THE LAW ABSTRACT PUBLISHING COMPANY, DBA THE OHIO PRINTING CO. LTD.

In 1979, the Association purchased the assets of the Ohio Printing Co. to gain greater control over the printing of its weekly magazine, the *Ohio State Bar Association*

Report. Ohio Printing is a for-profit, full-service Columbus printing company.

The Association is the company's largest customer but accounts for less than 25 percent of its total revenue. All of its directors are elected by the Association's Board of Governors.

In spring 2005, the OSBA Board of Governors decided to close the Ohio Printing Co. Because of ever-changing technologies, the use of alternative print vendors resulted in considerable savings for the Association.

OHIO LAWYERS ASSISTANCE PROGRAM INC.

Formed in the early '90s, the Ohio Lawyers Assistance Program is also a 501(c)(3) charitable organization. Its purpose is to help those practitioners who have alcohol or substance abuse problems. The staff remains small, taking calls from lawyers, their families and partners, and handling the organization's fund-raising efforts. The organization recently expanded its board of directors and is restructuring to meet the needs of those it serves.

Attorney Scott Mote, Columbus, manages this program for the Association.

OHIO STATE LEGAL SERVICES ASSOCIATION

This organization, established in 1966, provides civil legal services to those who are indigent and reside in any of 26 southeastern Ohio counties. The Ohio State Legal Services Association also offers support services, including training and publications, to legal services programs throughout Ohio. The Association appoints most of the attorney-members to the organization's board, but there are also non-attorney members. OSLSA receives most of its funding from the National Legal Services Corp. and from short-term trust accounts, called IOLTA accounts, that lawyers must maintain to hold clients' money.

Attorney Tom Weeks, Columbus, manages the Ohio State Legal Services Association.

chapter 23

Law Practice Today
... and Tomorrow

I N 2005, SOMEONE WHO OPENS A LAW OFFICE WITH a law degree, a shingle and a prayer, no matter how quick-witted or savvy, may easily become overwhelmed by issues without answers or research questions that cannot be resolved. He or she may need aid that is nowhere to be found. That is assuming he or she knows how to attract clients and how to keep them. Frustration, failure and even malpractice issues may not be far behind.

The more experienced attorney or one in a larger firm may not feel beleaguered so quickly or so often. But every now and again, there is bound to be that one question without an answer, that one concern that has not come up before.

It's the clever attorney who knows that a skilled legal mind is only as good as the resources supporting it. That's where today's Ohio State Bar Association makes the biggest difference.

The Association now includes 10 sections and 42 committees to provide support and address issues of a wide variety of practice areas. Most legal questions and knotty office issues can be handled by one of these.

Representatives of the 2004-2007 OSBA
Board of Governors:

Michael P. Hurley, Painesville
David C. Newcomer, Bryan
David E. Railsback, Mount Vernon

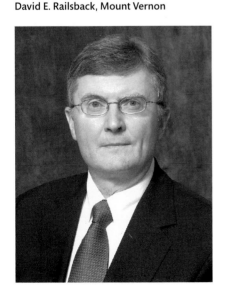

Representatives of the 2004–2007 OSBA
Board of Governors:

Robert F. Ware, Cleveland
Linda R. Warner, Pomeroy
Walter A. Wildman, Springfield

And to the future

"During the next 25 years, the Association will continue to provide specific membership value through advocacy and benefits," says Keith Ashmus, a partner in Frantz Ward, Cleveland, and president of the Association in 2003–2004. "And the staff is terrific, focused on the right things and not just 'what's in it for me.'"

Executive Director Denny Ramey agrees. "We listen to the needs of our members, we respond and we will continue to do so. We will do our best to keep ahead of the curve, so our members have cutting-edge advice, assistance and support."

Those with access to the Internet are now just a few clicks away from material that will make them smarter, better, more informed legal practitioners. Continuing legal education is there. The Web site, www.ohiobar.org, is there. *Ohio Lawyer* is there. Casemaker is there. Hot legislative topics are there.

The weekly *Ohio State Bar Association Report Online* includes all the materials of the *Ohio State Bar Association Report* and more. It's especially important for practitioners to keep up with the weekly report, since the Association and West Group are the state's "joint official reporters."

Committee and section meetings, Association district meetings, the annual meeting and continuing legal education courses bring information and up-to-the-minute material essential to law practice to all who seek it. A strong staff makes it all run well.

It is important for those outside the legal community to remember the people who make the clicks, write the briefs, argue the cases, meet the clients, resolve the issues, attend the educational sessions, help make the laws—and serve clients and other members of the public. Yes, lawyer jokes will continue, but there will also continue to be recognition of the good works of the profession.

As this publication is being prepared, the Association is initiating a "Future of the Profession" study—a comprehensive look at what the legal profession may resemble in the coming years, and how it will need to prepare to meet the needs of clients in the decades to come.

"The basic function of lawyers is always critical to any society," says the Hon. Richard Markus, who retired from Porter Wright Morris & Arthur, Cleveland, in 1998 and is now serving as a visiting common pleas judge.

"I'm truly proud of my profession," he says. "It provides leadership for almost all phases of our society. Law schools attract leaders, and train them to be leaders. The Bar Association then provides a mechanism for them to focus and use those talents."

Markus, who was president of the Association in 1991–1992, adds, "The manner in which attorneys provide services changes greatly—as society changes. Now, there are changes in technology, changes in communication and analysis. We can't predict what we will know, but we know that we will know it at a rapid rate. The Association, too, must keep pace with change. Society will always force adaptation to the developing new technology."

Still, he continues, some fundamentals will remain as long as there are laws and lawyers. "We remain responsible for guidance in troubled times, in conflict. And that," he concludes, "will always be the same."

OSBA Board of Governors: Front row: John S. Stith, Cincinnati; Sumner E. Walters, Lima; Michael B. Hendler, Akron; Heather G. Sowald, Columbus, OSBA president; Denny L. Ramey, Columbus, OSBA executive director; Reginald W. Jackson, Columbus; Walter A. Wildman, Springfield. Middle row: Linda R. Warner, Pomeroy; Lee E. Belardo, Avon; Stephen F. Tilson, Galion; Michael P. Hurley, Painesville; Ron L. Rimelspach, Sylvania; Gary L. Brown, Greenville; Richard C. Bannister, OSBA assistant executive director for administration. Back row: William K. Weisenberg, OSBA assistant executive director of public affairs and government relations; Robert F. Ware, Cleveland; David E. Railsback, Mount Vernon; David C. Newcomer, Bryan; Daniel P. Ruggiero, Portsmouth; Thomas P. Moushey, Alliance. Not pictured: E. Jane Taylor, Akron, OSBA president elect; Keith A. Ashmus, OSBA immediate past president; Shirley J. Christian, Youngstown; Mark A. Thomas, St. Clairsville.

"Over its 125-year history, and most certainly over the last 25 years, the Association has been one of the leading bar associations in the country," says Ramey. "It has done so by staying committed to a very simple, core goal: 'To be indispensable to Ohio lawyers.'"

"The key to our future is included in the pages of this book, as there are a number of excellent examples we can take forward in terms of how a bar association can play such a vital role in serving its members," he says.

E. Jane Taylor, Akron, representative of the 2000-2003 OSBA Board of Governors; OSBA president, 2004-2005.

Ramey speaks for the Association as a whole as he concludes, "Whether it's continued advances in technology, changes in how law is practiced in the future or legislative initiatives, staying focused on how the Association can serve Ohio lawyers and our ability to remain entrepreneurial in our thinking will keep us on the leading edge."

A look ahead

E. Jane Taylor, Akron, will become president of the Association on July 1, 2005. While this publication primarily offers a historical view, it is appropriate to include comments about the future from the incoming president of the Association.

"During my presidency, the Association will continue its tradition of being indispensable to lawyers by studying where the profession is headed in several key areas," Taylor says. "This will prepare us to deliver the support attorneys will need to continue their practices, to serve their clients and to support the legal needs of the public at large.

"What is old will be new again in the area of pro bono activities," she continues. "As the chief justice of the Supreme Court of Ohio and the American Bar Association commit to expanding and documenting pro bono services—and to informing people of those commitments—the Association will continue to work with its members and the organizations dedicated to providing underserved populations with the legal services they need."

She believes that "weaving diversity into the work of the bar and the growth of the profession will continue as a priority. Both a diversity policy and an action plan are in place. The face of the profession is changing to allow more and more people to see themselves as having access to and a stake in our system of justice.

"The future is bright for the legal profession, for the people it serves and for the Ohio State Bar Association."

And Taylor expresses the optimism of many members, staff and others involved in the organization as she concludes, "I'm looking forward to 2030—when the next chapter of the proud history of the Ohio State Bar Association will be chronicled in a special edition of *Buckeye Barristers* to be prepared for the 150th anniversary of this remarkable Association."

Ohio State Bar Association
Past Presidents

Year	President	Year	President	Year	President
1880	Rufus P. Ranney, Cleveland	1924	John A. Cline, Cleveland	1965	James F. Preston, Cleveland
1881	Rufus King, Cincinnati	1925	Province M. Pogue, Cincinnati	1966	Francis L. Dale, Cincinnati
1882	R. A. Harrison, Columbus	1926	Hon. John M. McCabe, Toledo	1967	Norton R. Webster, Columbus
1883	Durbin Ward, Cincinnati	1927	Charles B. Hunt, Coshocton	1968	Robert D. Moss, Barberton
1884	A. W. Jones, Youngstown	1928	Jon A. Elden, Cleveland	1969	Bitner Browne, Springfield
1885	W. J. Gilmore, Columbus	1929	William G. Pickrel, Dayton	1970	Merritt W. Green, Toledo
1886	John A. McMahon, Dayton	1930	Phil S. Bradford, Columbus	1971	Myron W. Ulrich, Cleveland
1887	E. P. Green, Akron	1931	Walter A. Ryan, Cincinnati	1972	Rudolph Janata, Columbus
1888	J. J. Moore, Ottawa	1932	Robert Guinther, Akron	1973	Walter A. Porter, Dayton
1889	J. T. Holmes, Columbus	1933	A. R. Johnson, Ironton	1974	William L. Howland, Portsmouth
1890	Henderson Elliott, Dayton	1934	George W. Spooner, Cleveland	1975	Daniel I. Rosenthal, Springfield
1891	Samuel F. Hunt, Cincinnati	1935	Charles W. Racine, Toledo	1976	Jamille G. Jamra, Toledo
1892	John H. Doyle, Toledo	1936	George R. Murray, Dayton	1977	Sam D. Bartlo, Akron
1893	Stephen R. Harris, Bucyrus	1937	Walter S. Ruff, Canton	1978	John M. Adams, Columbus
1894	Charles Pratt, Toledo	1938	Howard L. Barkdull, Cleveland	1979	Joseph A. Oths, Wellston
1895	John J. Hall, Akron	1939	Gerritt J. Fredriks, Cincinnati	1980	Loren E. Souers, Canton
1896	George K. Nash, Columbus	1940	Donald A. Finkbeiner, Toledo	1981	John A. Howard, Elyria
1897	Judson Harmon, Hillsboro	1941	Chester G. Wise, Akron	1982	Norman W. Shibley, Cleveland
1898	Virgil P. Kline, Cleveland	1942	Andrew S. Iddings, Dayton	1983	John A. Carnahan, Columbus
1899	Peter A. Laubie, Salem	1943	Waymon B. McLeskey, Columbus	1984	Frank E. Bazler, Troy
1900	R. D. Marshall, Dayton	1944	Jay P. Taggart, Cleveland	1985	Duke W. Thomas, Columbus
1901	S. S. Wheeler, Lima	1945	Jay P. Taggart, Cleveland	1986	Leslie W. Jacobs, Cleveland
1902	John W. Warington, Cincinnati	1946	Howard F. Guthery, Marion	1987	Joseph F. Cook, Akron
1903	Henry J. Booth, Columbus	1947	Joseph D. Stecher, Toledo	1988	Joseph T. Svete, Chardon
1904	James O. Troup, Bowling Green	1948	Philip C. Ebeling, Dayton	1989	Robert A. McCarthy, Troy
1905	Edward Kibler, Newark	1949	James M. Hengst, Columbus	1990	Gerald L. Draper, Columbus
1906	John C. Hale, Cleveland	1950	Hon. Paul C. Weick, Akron	1991	Richard M. Markus, Cleveland
1907	Thomas B. Paxton, Cincinnati	1951	Ben C. Boer, Cleveland	1992	H. Ritchey Hollenbaugh, Columbus
1908	A. D. Follett, Marietta	1952	Harry S. Wonnell, Hamilton	1993	Kathleen B. Burke, Cleveland
1909	Jerome B. Burrows, Painesville	1953	C. Kenneth Clark, Youngstown	1994	Ray R. Michalski, Lancaster
1910	Allen Andrews, Hamilton	1954	John C. Durfey, Springfield	1995	James R. Jeffery, Toledo
1911	Frederick L. Taft, Cleveland	1955	Fred A. Smith, Toledo	1996	John B. Robertson, Cleveland
1912	Simeon M. Johnson, Cincinnati	1956	Earl F. Morris, Columbus	1997	Thomas M. Taggart, Columbus
1913	Harlan F. Burket, Findlay	1957	Aronhold C. Schapiro, Portsmouth	1998	John P. Petzold, Dayton
1914	John H. Van Deman, Dayton	1958	William R. Van Aken, Cleveland	1999	Thomas J. Bonasera, Columbus
1915	Charles R. Miller, Cleveland	1959	Allan B. Diefenbach, Akron	2000	Reginald S. Jackson Jr., Toledo
1916	Edmund B. King, Sandusky	1960	Matthew J. Smith, New Philadelphia	2001	Mary Jane Trapp, Cleveland
1917	John A. Shauck, Dayton	1961	John C. Johnston Jr., Wooster	2002	Stephen E. Chappelear, Columbus
1918	Ensign N. Brown, Youngstown	1962	Lawrence J. Burns, Coshocton	2003	Keith A. Ashmus, Cleveland
1919	Smith W. Bennet, Bucyrus	1963	Erle H. Bridgewater Jr., Athens	2004	Heather G. Sowald, Columbus
1920	Daniel W. Iddings, Dayton	1964	Roger H. Smith, Toledo	2005	E. Jane Taylor, Akron
1921	Curtis E. McBride, Mansfield				
1922	George B. Harris, Cleveland				
1923	Hon. William L. Hart, Alliance				

*about
the
author*

*Julia L. Osborne, Esq., is a
Columbus, Ohio, native who
practices immigration law and is a
freelance writer for newspapers,
magazines and professional
organizations. She is a member of
the Ohio State Bar Association and
the American Bar Association as
well as the American Immigration
Lawyers Association.*